TEENS &
LIBRARIES
Getting It Right

Virginia A. Walter ▬▬▬ Elaine Meyers

American Library Association
Chicago   2003

While extensive effort has gone into ensuring the reliability of information appearing in this book, the publisher makes no warranty, express or implied, on the accuracy or reliability of the information, and does not assume and hereby disclaims any liability to any person for any loss or damage caused by errors or omissions in this publication.

Design and composition by ALA Editions in Berkeley Book and ITC Legacy Sans Book using QuarkXPress 5 on a PC platform

Printed on 50-pound white offset, a pH-neutral stock, and bound in 10-point cover stock by Victor Graphics

The paper used in this publication meets the minimum requirements of American National Standard for Information Sciences—Permanence of Paper for Printed Library Materials, ANSI Z39.48-1992. ∞

Library of Congress Cataloging-in-Publication Data

Walter, Virginia A.
    Teens and libraries : getting it right / Virginia A. Walter, Elaine E. Meyers.
        p.   cm.
    Includes bibliographical references and index.
    ISBN 0-8389-0857-8 (alk. paper)
    1. Young adults' libraries—United States. 2. Libraries and teenagers—United States. 3. Teenagers—Books and reading—United States. 4. Young adult services librarians—United States. I. Meyers, Elaine E. II. Title.
    Z718.5.W36 2003
    027.62′6—dc21   2003009292

Printed in the United States of America

07   06   05   04   03   5   4   3   2   1

Contents

PART FOUR

Toolkit

Foreword

In *Teens and Libraries: Getting It Right,* Virginia Walter and Elaine Meyers have captured our history, challenged us to implement new concepts, and asked us to make and keep new promises to youth and our profession. This very readable book is a call to action in many ways. The authors ask us to reflect on our past, learn from the best research and practice available today, and work within our communities to create a new future for youth.

The American Library Association and the Urban Libraries Council are proud to have collaborated on many aspects leading to the publication of this book. Our mutual support for research, professional publications, and librarians in the field make us allies and advocates for partnerships at all levels. We believe with the authors that the roles played by libraries in strengthening communities through work with city and county governments, private and public institutions, and grassroots organizations not only reflect our past but ensure our future as vital community organizations.

The belief that teens can make a difference in our libraries and communities mandates that we work with teens in our libraries to provide the kind of spaces, services, and opportunities needed for their successful passage into adulthood. We enjoy the challenges of today's teens and applaud their desire to create new worlds using technology in new and insightful ways. We are happy to build the future with them—a future they will inherit. We also foresee some of these teens replacing us professionally, and we renew our commitment to mentor and nourish the next generation of public librarians and community leaders.

ELEANOR JO (JOEY) RODGER
President, Urban Libraries Council

CARLA HAYDEN
President, American Library Association 2003–2004
Executive Director, Enoch Pratt Free Library

v

Preface

We have been involved with teens and libraries in one way or another for most of our long library careers. We have been young adult librarians and consultants to libraries trying to develop better services for teens. Ginny wrote *Output Measures and More: Planning and Evaluating Public Library Services for Young Adults* for the Young Adult Library Services Association, and Elaine served on the advisory board for that project. Elaine was the project director for the Public Libraries as Partners in Youth Development (PLPYD) project, which was funded by the Wallace–Reader's Digest Fund and administered by the Urban Libraries Council, and Ginny served on the national advisory committee for the evaluation of that project. Ginny now teaches future youth services librarians in the Information Studies Department at the University of California, Los Angeles (UCLA), while Elaine supervises services for children and young adults at the Burton Barr Central Library in Phoenix, Arizona.

Over the years, we have found ourselves telling each other stories about our work. These stories had heroes: irrepressible teens, gifted library administrators, remarkable library school students, and dedicated librarians—and villains: professionals who romanticized the past and resisted change, bureaucrats in all kinds of settings, and library leaders who blew their chances to make a difference. We found ourselves looking for the stories of our past, digging into library history for clues to the present and pathways to the future. We have also devoted a lot of time to analyzing and interpreting the narratives that are told by the teens of today and the librarians and other adults who care about them.

Most recently, our stories have sprung from the PLPYD initiative. This book was funded as part of the effort to disseminate the knowledge gained from that project. We found that the PLPYD story was embedded in a much larger narrative about the past, present, and future of public library services for teens in the United States. This is the story we share with you in this book.

Part 1 of this book is a historical chronicle, the stories our predecessors and peers have taught us about public libraries and teens. It takes us from the innovation of young adult library services in the 1920s through the golden age of the 1930s and 1940s to the problematic conditions at the end of the twentieth century. Part 2 is best understood as a series of counter-stories to the traditional narrative in part 1. It presents the learning from the PLPYD project and takes it further, giving readers a glimpse of a possible second golden age to come. Finally, in part 3, we present what academics might call a "metanarrative." It is the story that we have developed by rereading and synthesizing the traditional story in part 1 and the counter-stories in part 2. Our metanarrative is presented in the form of promises we want to make to the young adults of tomorrow and a strategy for keeping those promises. The last section, part 4, is a toolkit or manual that provides you with some practical aids to help you write the story of young adult services in your own community and keep your own promises to the teens who live there.

Getting it right for teens and libraries, however, involves much more than following the manual or even knowing the rules. Getting it right means understanding our roles as adults and professionals. Getting it right requires a genuine commitment to youth participation. Getting it right is about shifting our perspective from the library to the community in which it is located. Getting it right makes it imperative that we give teens a place of their own in our libraries. And getting it right obliges us to acquire the skills and knowledge we need to institutionalize young adult services and ensure their sustainability.

The titles we have given to each major section of this book have their own significance. We have chosen to recognize some of the classics of young adult literature in the part titles. S. E. Hinton, the first young adult author who was herself a young adult when she began to write, transformed this genre by writing in a voice that her teen readers would understand to be absolutely authentic. We have chosen her novel *That Was Then, This Is Now* for part 1, in which we tell the early and recent history of public library services for teens in the United States. Hinton's *Rumble Fish*, a story of inclusion and exclusion, seemed just right for part 2, with its clamor of new voices telling new stories. Finally, we have invoked her finest novel, *The Outsiders,* for part 3. This is a novel that has special meaning for us. In the late 1970s, Ginny read it out loud, a chapter at a time, to the young Latino gang members who came to her library in Boyle Heights, in Los Angeles. They were riveted by this story of white boys in Oklahoma whose values, experiences, and code of honor were so similar to their own. Almost twenty years later, she ran into one of them again. "Hey, do you remember when you used to read to us about Ponyboy and them?" asked Julio. He had been profoundly touched by the power of the narrative. Julio had also been brought inside the circle of library users by the experience of hearing it read out loud by an adult who cared about him. We find that teens today still respond to Hinton's story of family bonds and class divisions. Almost all teenagers feel like outsiders when they approach a public library. Our goal is to make them feel like insiders, as comfortable in the library domain as they are in more common teen hangouts.

We want to acknowledge the Wallace–Reader's Digest Fund for its support. We also want to thank the teens and UCLA students who have inspired us—and many insightful, committed colleagues at the American Library Association, the Urban Libraries Council, PLPYD project sites, the Forum for Youth Investment, and the Chapin Hall Center for Children at the University of Chicago. All of you have informed our thinking and contributed to the ongoing narrative of teens and libraries. All of you have worked to get it right.

This is a story with an open ending. We invite you to read it. Retell it and talk about it with the teens in your community and the adults who care about them. Enlist them all as coauthors as you collaborate to write the next chapter with your own words and deeds.

· VIRGINIA WALTER
ELAINE MEYERS

PART ONE

That Was Then, This Is Now

The two chapters in part 1 provide the background story of young adult services in American libraries. These are the stories our predecessors and peers have told us. The protagonists are the architects of young adult services—strong women like Amelia Munson and Margaret A. Edwards—and the youth advocates of the late twentieth century. The prevailing metaphor for part 1 is architectural. We found that the story of young adult services is really a subplot in the story of public library services in this country. Public libraries and young adult services are both built on a foundation with three pillars: reading, information and education, and community. These pillars are not equal, however, and often the institution on which they are built has tilted one way or another. Sometimes we envision the public library as a tipsy three-legged stool; at other times, it seems like a glorious temple with Corinthian columns. Either way, part 1 is about the foundations.

Social scientists talk about institution-building, the process by which people create organizations or services in those organizations that persist over time. Scholars have identified what is needed to institutionalize an organization or service or even an idea. These include a compelling mission, leaders who can articulate the mission compellingly, a structure for carrying out the mission, and, most importantly, the ability to build strong linkages with the community or environment (Gladwell 2000; Selznick 1957). When we look at the narrative of young adult library services—then and now—as told in the next two chapters, we see that it is a story of institution-building. The institution builders of young adult services have not always been successful, and we will try to understand why as we develop a new approach for the next golden age.

CHAPTER 1

Where We Came From

We begin our quest for the future of young adult library services in the past, searching for our roots. What we have discovered from digging into library history is that services for young adults have not followed a linear track. There is no tidy path of progress, no clear and continuous trajectory from the past to the present. Instead the chronology is fragmented and discontinuous, characterized by long periods of inactivity punctuated by sporadic upturns of energy and interest. Still, the story bears repeating because it contains some important lessons that inform and underlie our conviction that a radical change is needed in our thinking about teens and libraries.

The story makes the most sense as a history of ideas. Specifically, it is a story of three different ideas about the nature of public library service. Sometimes these ideas have coexisted; sometimes they have competed with each other. These ideas have been championed by leaders in the profession. They have endured because they were codified and disseminated by articulate, influential writers and speakers. Different ideas have been dominant at different times in American library history. Each of these ideas, or visions, about what the public library should be has affected the ways in which librarians have understood their jobs and the ways in which young adults were served.

Perhaps the most familiar idea is that of the public library as an institution where reading is promoted and where readers are nurtured. The second idea is that of the library as an educational institution, often linked with the need for an informed citizenry. The third idea is more abstract, envisioning the library as a force for the community good with a responsibility for contributing to the betterment of society.

In this chapter, we will look briefly at each of these three ideas about the mission of the public library, with a special emphasis on their earliest manifestations in library discourse, and relate it to developments in young adult services over time. We will end this initial historical chronicle with the year 1969 and the publication of Margaret Edwards's seminal book, *The Fair Garden and the Swarm of Beasts,* and finally look back at the factors creating our first golden age of modern young adult services.

LIBRARIES FOR READERS

The first American public libraries were established in the second half of the nineteenth century by civic-minded elites in New England towns. The intent of these early library supporters was to make the benefits of reading available to those who could not afford to buy their own books—not just any books, but good books. Cheap reading material such as dime novels and light romances was widely available to the lower classes. The purpose of the public library was to provide more uplifting literature that would edify and educate its readers (Molz and Dain 1999, 11). The policymakers charged with developing a mission for the new Boston Public Library in 1852 put it this way: "There can be no doubt that . . . reading ought to be furnished to all, on the same principle that we furnish free education" (Williams 1988, 4).

From the beginning, however, there were librarians who were more pragmatic about the reading interests of their clientele. They recognized that many people would not come eagerly or willingly to some of the more difficult and demanding works of literature. The strategy for reaching these readers would be to supply them with popular fiction first. Then when they had acquired a reading and library habit, they would be weaned from the light novels to more substantial fare. The Boston trustees, in their mission statement, described this process as a kind of taste elevation, and claimed that the effectiveness of this process was a matter of common knowledge. It just made sense to them that readers would progress to fine literature if they were exposed to it.

The theory of taste elevation in readers had its detractors. Some critics asserted that it didn't work, that readers of light novels continued to be readers of light novels. Some public libraries refused to stock any kind of fiction, considering it to be too seductive to their readers. The result, of course, tended to be a decrease in library usage. As early as 1883, some librarians were questioning the very premise that libraries ought to provide only fine, uplifting literature. At the American Library Association (ALA) Conference that year, Mellen Chamberlain, then the head of the Boston Public Library, made the argument that since public taxes supported the library, public demand in reading material ought to be honored (Williams 1988, 18). That same year, the fiery Tessa Kelso, head of the Los Angeles Public Library, asserted that librarians had a mandate to provide recreation as well as education. She pointed out that libraries' most important contribution to society might be to provide opportunities and resources for relaxation and pleasure (Williams 1988, 20).

In this early controversy, we recognize the framework of the ongoing debate about "quality versus demand" theories of collection development. Few public libraries reject the notion of providing popular materials to adults today; in fact, best-sellers are the bedrock of the adult collection in most branch libraries. Today it is primarily youth services librarians who still base many of their services on the principle of "taste elevation," delivering "bait and switch" book talks in the hopes of leading readers from trash or trivia to the good stuff. A conviction that books and reading are essential to the human condition is so ingrained in the library profession that in 1950 Robert D. Leigh called it the library faith, "a belief in the virtue of the printed word, especially of the book, the reading of which is held to be good in itself or from its reading flows that which is good" (Leigh 1950, 12).

The Carnegie libraries, built throughout the country from 1886 to 1917, were designed to make the circulation of reading materials efficient. Abigail Van Slyck documents how the designs for these buildings, which were approved by officials at the Carnegie Corporation before the money was released to local communities, moved from closed to open stacks and an open floor plan that made supervision of readers easy to manage. This was all part of a philosophy that James Bertram, Carnegie's personal secretary, called "effectiv library accommodation" (Van Slyck 1995, 35). Note the use of Melvil Dewey's "simplified spelling." Most of the Carnegie libraries were also furnished with circulation desks and other furniture supplied by the Library Bureau, a business that Dewey had established in order to implement the best professional practices in libraries.

Van Slyck finds that the Carnegie focus on library efficiency even influenced how public libraries came to perceive their mission. Before the Carnegie library became the paradigmatic model for public library buildings after the turn of the century, many public libraries had seen themselves as multipurpose institutions designed to foster many forms of cultural and intellectual expression. They had auditoriums and meeting rooms where people came together to hear speakers and discuss ideas. Some even had attached museums. Now, under the influence of the principle of "effectiv library accommodation" and the funding that came with it, public libraries became more interested in putting books quickly into the hands of individual, solitary readers. The circulation desk became the focal point that symbolized the library (Van Slyck 1995, 219–20).

Interestingly, Carnegie libraries allocated space for children and thus contributed to the general institutionalization of public library services for children. Bertram initially tried to enforce guidelines for children's rooms that created scaled-down versions of adult reading rooms, with orderly rows of tables and chairs designed to foster orderly reading behavior. Early on, however, children's librarians adopted the progressive and child-oriented philosophy of psychologist G. Stanley Hall and educator John Dewey, and they were able to modify Bertram's guidelines and create more child-friendly environments (Van Slyck 1995, 175ff). There is no record of any designated space for older children—teens or young adults—in the Carnegie building plans.

Amelia Munson Sets the Challenge

Amelia Munson was not the first young adult librarian. That distinction is traditionally accorded to Mabel Williams, who began as head of the School Work Department at the New York Public Library (NYPL) in 1919 (Braverman 1979). However, Munson followed Williams as the head of young adult services in New York and took the time to reflect and write about this specialization in a book published by the American Library Association in 1950. *An Ample Field: Books and Young People* takes its title from a quote by Chaucer: "I have, God knows, an ample field to plow and feeble oxen." This would seem to indicate the challenge Munson had taken on: to provide a stronger team and better tools for those few librarians working to connect teens with books.

In both the subtitle and the foreword to *An Ample Field*, Munson makes it clear that young adult librarians are indeed "working in the field of young people's reading" (Munson 1950, vii). Later she acknowledges that not all teens are readers. She recognizes that some who were avid readers as children had now become too busy with other distractions or had been seduced by the easy charms of radio, television, movies, or comics. Some had not mastered the mechanics of reading sufficiently to experience its pleasures. Others had been turned off by being given inappropriate books, while still others read indiscriminately, without judgment. A few, of course, are "natural and devoted readers." Munson advises the young adult librarian to find common ground with all of these (Munson 1950, 9).

Why bother to lead reluctant teens to books? Munson devotes an entire chapter to justifying the work of attracting young people to books. She abandons the usual canon of lofty rationales—to gain perspective, broaden horizons, acquire culture, etc.—in favor of four reasons that are more firmly grounded in the reality of voluntary reading: the satisfaction of curiosity, pure relaxation, the necessity of escape, and the propinquity or availability of reading material. And it's all for enjoyment. "Greater than all is the one encompassing phrase, 'the pursuit of happiness.' Reading for fun is the main thing; one sometimes wonders if reading without enjoyment accomplishes anything except the creation of distaste for the whole process" (Munson 1950, 17).

The way to stimulate this enjoyment in teen readers was to understand all of the many interests they might have and then find books that reflect those interests. Because the field of specialized young adult publishing did not yet exist in 1950, the young adult librarian was expected to read widely from the books published for both children and adults and then select the most readable and suitable to introduce to teens (Munson 1950, 10–11).

While Amelia Munson wrote the first handbook for young adult librarians, one that clearly focused on the importance of the library in promoting books and reading, her influence was not as enduring as that of Margaret A. Edwards, a charismatic and dogmatic woman whose career spanned several decades at the Enoch Pratt Free Library in Baltimore. Margaret Edwards reinforced the idea that library service to young adults was all about reading.

Margaret Edwards Codifies Library Services for the Teen Reader

Margaret A. Edwards was hired in 1933 by the legendary Joseph L. Wheeler to set up a program for library work with young adults in Baltimore (Edwards 1974, 13). She paid an early visit to the New York Public Library to see what that pioneering library was doing with teens. She liked much of what she saw. She used the NYPL book lists as a basis for training staff and for building collections at Enoch Pratt, and ultimately adopted the NYPL innovation of the book talk as a cornerstone of young adult services there. In an interview with Mary Kay Chelton much later, Edwards expressed disapproval, however, of one NYPL branch where the librarian had enticed "juvenile delinquents" into the library with chess and board games. "This was the one activity I observed that I could not accept," she said (Campbell 1998, 23).

When she began working at Enoch Pratt, Edwards realized that as a former high school teacher she knew something about the young people who were her patrons but very little about the books they should read. She embarked on a determined effort to overcome this limitation, reading in streetcars, on buses, on her lunch hour, and in her dentist's waiting room. She took recommendations from young adults as well and began to assemble collections based on her newly acquired knowledge. She also began an aggressive campaign to promote the books to her young patrons, providing a level of reading guidance that apparently shocked her coworkers. Very early in her career, she formulated a philosophy of work with young adults that she claimed was as simple as ABC: "(A) a sympathetic understanding of all adolescents; (B) firsthand knowledge of all the books that would interest them; and (C) mastery of the technique of getting these books into the hands of adolescents" (Edwards 1974, 16).

Edwards had no research findings to back up her passionate belief that literature and great ideas in great books could change young lives for the better. She had, however, a wealth of personal experience and her own clinical observations of the young people she saw in the library. From this knowledge base she developed the theory that librarians could do nothing better than to develop young adults' reading habits and tastes. The atomic bombing of Hiroshima in 1945 convinced her of the gap between man's technical knowledge and his emotional and cultural development. She ardently believed that the library could help to reduce this gap. "More young people needed to come to the library for voluntary reading and those who came should be introduced to better and better books until they were reading with enjoyment in an ever-widening range of stimulating and inspiring subjects" (Edwards 1974, 19).

In her quest for books that would not just inform young people but actually change their lives, Edwards was vehemently opposed to censorship. She insisted that young people should read about life as it is, not how we want it to be. She was remarkably open-minded for her time about the need for young people to read about sex, not just informational books but novels that "go beyond the facts to the emotional implications of love" (Edwards 1974, 72). In her book *Youth, Society, and the Public Library*, Miriam Braverman includes the text of a lengthy memo that Edwards wrote to the director of the Pratt Library arguing for teen access to *Lady Chatterley's Lover*. Edwards wrote, "Of course, a frank description of sexual intercourse is going to offend people who do not wish sex to be referred to, but the book is of such unquestioned standing in the literary world and is so obviously sincere, it seems to me less likely to be harmful than are many titles, now available to teen-agers, which are overdrawn, satirical, or sometimes brutal novels of only fair merit" (Braverman 1979, 191). Edwards was also remarkably candid in her writings about her own early repression and sexual awakening when, at the age of forty, she married a man who taught her that sex was normal and fulfilling.

The only way that librarians could introduce better and better books to young people was by knowing the books themselves. As the supervisor of work for young adults at Enoch Pratt, Edwards required her assistants to read 300 books considered suitable for teens. As they read each batch of ten, they came into her office to discuss them with her, one on one (Edwards 1974, 22).

It is amusing to read Edwards's own accounts of the resistance to the reading program she prescribed, both by the young assistants and their line supervisors in the branch libraries. Edwards, of course, was undaunted by the reluctance of some of her colleagues to support her aggressive program of continuing education and professional development. She felt that her critics just weren't real professionals. "A professional," she wrote, "is not a blue-collar worker who punches a clock. He works when he is needed and he renews himself constantly. This renewal by reading is generally overlooked by librarians, old and young" (Edwards 1974, 87). Indeed, Edwards was critical of the library profession as a whole, finding most of its practitioners to be colorless personalities who are only interested in organizing and administering a book collection with as little contact with patrons as possible.

Edwards expected her assistants to put their book knowledge to work on the floor of the library. She was scathing in her criticism of those passive librarians who simply sat at their desks, only stirring themselves to point in the general direction of a book desired by a patron. The librarians trained by Edwards were on their feet, approaching their young patrons with friendly, helpful tips about books to read. These librarians were expected to act their age. "Nothing distresses the young adult more than the sight of an adult attempting to be young again" (Edwards 1974, 20). Edwards also anticipated contemporary library approaches to customer service, looking at successful retail clerks as models for satisfying patron needs (Edwards 1974, 25ff).

At regular staff meetings, the librarians continued to discuss books and techniques for getting them in the hands of young adults. Edwards raised the book annotation to an art form. In an appendix to her book, *The Fair Garden and the Swarm of Beasts,* she includes samples of annotations that are "merely adequate" and those written with art (Edwards 1974, 153). One suspects that she herself wrote the "artful" examples.

Edwards also championed the book talk as a way to introduce teens to good books. She outlined five objectives in giving book talks to teenagers:

1. To sell the idea of reading for pleasure
2. To introduce new ideas and new fields of reading

3. To develop appreciation of style and character portrayal
4. To lift the level of reading by introducing the best books the audience can read with pleasure
5. To humanize books, the library, and the librarian (Edwards 1974, 155–56)

Just as she had firm ideas about what makes an excellent annotation, Edwards had high standards for book talks. She offers no fewer than twenty tips for effective book talk delivery, but also reminds the librarian that she is not on trial as a performer but as a promoter of reading. She insisted that the true test of one's effectiveness as a booktalker should be the number of young people who check out the books that have been highlighted (Edwards 1974, 157–60).

Margaret Edwards was not the first young adult librarian. She did not even write the first book about young adult services. But she was perhaps the most influential codifier of young adult library services. She published *The Fair Garden and the Swarm of Beasts: The Library and the Young Adult,* a compilation of her writings on the subject, in 1969, at the end of her career. She revised the book in 1974; and the American Library Association reissued it, with a long foreword by Patty Campbell, in 1994. In 2002, on the centennial of Edwards's birth, yet another edition appeared, this one with an informative foreword by Betty Carter (2002) that analyzes Edwards's contributions in light of current trends in young adult library services. *The Fair Garden and the Swarm of Beasts* has a broader scope than Munson's book, combining personal memoirs, discussions of best practice, and a well-defined philosophy of service for teen library users. It continues to inspire contemporary young adult librarians and to inform their practice.

The focus on books that was first articulated by Amelia Munson and then codified by Margaret A. Edwards is reflected today in the continuing cultivation of the art of the book talk by young adult librarians and by the recognition given to books by the Young Adult Library Services Association. The association has produced lists of the Best Books for Young Adults for many years and has honored Margaret Edwards with an award in her honor, given each year to an author of young adult literature for a body of work.

The tradition of public library service to young adults has its deepest roots in the idea of the public library as a provider of books and reading. However, the idea of the library as an educational institution has also played a role in the development of young adult services.

LIBRARIES AS EDUCATIONAL INSTITUTIONS

As the twentieth century dawned, many public librarians had become disenchanted with their role, whether they saw it as elevating the reading taste of their patrons or as offering recreational resources and opportunities. The first role seemed futile while the second appeared trivial. Patrick Williams writes that librarians redeemed their sense of purpose by adopting a new and militant fervor for education. In particular, they would educate the masses of immigrants swarming to our shores. They would teach these newcomers to be good Americans. They would not rely solely on uplifting books to achieve this objective, although they did seek out books in the languages spoken by the new immigrants and books dealing with the practical issues facing them. In addition, however, they would provide classes in English, citizenship, and the American way of life. Perhaps infected by the optimism that was widespread during this era of progressivism, public librarians committed themselves to a "library spirit" that they believed would sweep the land.

We can see two ways in which the idea of the public library as an educational institution was implemented. One was as a support to individuals' formal education; the other was as a resource for independent learners.

Public Libraries as a Support to Formal Education

Ideally, formal educational institutions—schools—maintain their own libraries to support the learning of their students. While public libraries have sometimes been reluctant to take on a role that could be seen to duplicate that of school and college libraries, they have often seen the need or the desirability of augmenting those services. Since most young adults are also secondary school students, young adult librarians have traditionally sought ways to support their learning. In fact, the first formal public library services for young adults identified high school students as their primary customers.

MABEL WILLIAMS CREATES PUBLIC LIBRARY SERVICES FOR TEEN STUDENTS

When Mabel Williams was hired by Anne Carroll Moore in 1919 to develop young adult library services at the New York Public Library, she began by targeting high school students. Service to teens would focus on building relationships with the schools where many fourteen- to eighteen-year-olds spent their days. This focus on schools was a natural extension of the philosophy of service to children that Moore had already established. By the 1930s, however, it also came in line with national policies geared to adolescents.

In 1935 President Roosevelt had established the National Youth Administration (NYA) with Aubrey Williams as its head. One of the programs established by the NYA created jobs for high school students whose families were on relief, jobs that paid six dollars a month for as much as twenty hours of work a week. These salaries were set deliberately low in order to discourage young people from dropping out of school. Rather, they were intended to provide an incentive for poor kids to stay in school by paying for the modest shoes and clothing that allowed them to face their more economically advantaged peers (Hine 1999, 206ff). Admittedly, the goal of the NYA was not so much to keep teens in school as to keep them out of the workforce where the few available jobs were needed for heads of households. The program did result in increased high school enrollments; high school attendance soared during the Depression. By 1936, 65 per cent of all teenagers were high school students, the greatest proportion of American youth to enroll in secondary school up to that time (Palladino 1996, 5).

At the NYPL, Mabel Williams spent the Depression years recruiting sympathetic staff—called school and reference assistants—to help ease these increasing numbers of high school students from the comfort and familiarity of the children's room to the larger and more complex collections and services of the adult departments. The teens needed friendly faces; many of the longtime reference librarians were hostile to these new patrons who were neither children nor adults. Williams described the problems she had with older librarians who felt that high school students should do their work in their school libraries instead of annoying adults at the public library. "They [the teens] were not welcomed, and there was no attempt to have books that related to their interests. The adult librarians felt no obligation to know what their interests were and to be able to recommend books, until we started the work" (Braverman 1979, 33).

Outreach to schools was the focus of young adult work at the NYPL throughout the Depression years. Teachers were invited to bring their classes to the library for book talks and library instruction that were designed to increase the students' comfort and competence in using the adult collection for their homework. The public librarians created recommended book lists that they shared with teachers and encouraged them to use with their students.

Public library outreach to high schools and support for their students appeared to dwindle dramatically after World War II. The release of the publications comprising the Public Library Inquiry (PLI) may also have contributed to a retreat from the educational function that formed the basis of much young adult service at that time. The Public Library Inquiry was intended to provide research-based evidence on which decision-makers could redefine and revitalize the institution of the public library. Patrick Williams (1988, 66) points out that Robert D. Leigh's *The Public Library in the United States,* the publication that summarized the findings of the PLI, blasted the notion that public libraries could ever be an effective instrument of popular education. The book's failure to document or comment on public libraries' services to young people may also have had a dampening effect on postwar young adult services in general.

Interestingly, however, teens continued to use the public library for homework materials and a place to study in spite of the library's evident dismissal of their educational needs. When the numbers of teens surged in the 1960s, public libraries reported being overrun by hordes of students (Williams 1988, 94; Molz and Dain 1999, 17). In some libraries, this actually created a backlash against the teens who were crowding out adult patrons. By the 1960s, the "student problem" was perceived to be so out of hand that many public libraries started limiting their services to students. In some cases reference service to teens was curtailed or denied altogether (Mediavilla, "Why Library Homework Centers," 2001). Responding to teens' educational needs was not seen as a priority by public libraries again until the late 1990s, when homework assistance programs began to crop up throughout the country. We will address this development in our next chapter.

Public Libraries as Supports for Independent Learners

Public library support for independent learners was often couched in terms of providing information to individuals. Teens have not often been perceived as having individual and independent learning needs; their identity as high school students tends to be the dominant one.

Braverman's case study (1979, 148ff) of youth services at the Cleveland Public Library, however, documents an early—and apparently anomalous—effort to serve teens who had left school to join the workforce. The Stevenson Room at the Cleveland Public Library was established in 1926 to serve adolescents. Unlike other pioneering young adult library programs that focused their efforts solely on high school students, the Cleveland model consciously addressed the needs of out-of-school youth. Jean Roos, the first director of the Stevenson Room, prepared a "new job card" for teens who had been issued work permits. The card encouraged these young people to go to their local library for vocational information. Braverman also reports on book discussion groups for young factory workers and shop girls in the late 1920s and the establishment of deposit collections in National Youth Administration offices.

There is also some documentation that teens at the NYPL during the 1930s and 1940s were seen as independent learners with individual learning goals and needs, rather than simply as students with homework assignments. Braverman reports that librarians in the branches began at that time to create browsing collections and special spaces for teens—lounges where young adults could relax with board games or knit or just talk with friends. Many of the libraries started clubs for teens where they could study African-American history, read plays, play chess, learn about current events, talk about books, and pursue many other interests.

It is relatively easy to document public library services designed to advance the library's mission to promote reading or to provide educational and information resources. The function of the public library as a support for democracy and as a force for community betterment is a little more abstract and more difficult to isolate. Nevertheless, it is important to account for this idea because it too affected public library ideology and services to teens.

LIBRARIES FOR THE COMMUNITY GOOD

In the remarkable document that laid out the objectives for the Boston Public Library in 1852, the founding trustees were unequivocal about the civic benefits that would result from the establishment of this publicly supported institution. They acknowledged that the library would supply books for the great masses of people who could not afford to buy them. By doing so, they intended to "affect life and raise personal character and condition" (*Upon the Objects* 1852, 20). This mission was important, however, not just because it would raise the conditions of individuals but because it would bolster the very foundations of our democratic society. Here is how the trustees expressed it, in the flowery language of nineteenth-century educated men:

> For it has been rightly judged that,—under political, social and religious institutions like ours,—it is of paramount importance that the means of general information should be so diffused that the largest possible number of persons should be induced to read and understand questions going down to the very foundations of social order, which are constantly presenting themselves, and which we, as a people are constantly required to decide, and do decide, either ignorantly, or wisely. (*Upon the Objects* 1852, 15)

From this one complex sentence, we can see that from its very beginnings the American public library was linked to the development of the informed citizenry that was deemed essential to an effective democracy. Later in its history, this would be manifested by the library profession's passionate advocacy of the First Amendment right to intellectual freedom and its opposition to censorship.

The Civic Dimensions of Young Adult Library Services

There is a strong civic element in the passionate humanism of the early advocates for young adult services. Mabel Williams, Margaret Edwards, and Jean Roos, in particular, appear to have been women who were closely engaged with the political and social events of their times. In their writing and in their implementation of library services for teens, they often linked reading with the individual's development of positive social values. In some cases, they provided programming that reinforced those values.

The Roads to World Understanding program was a joint venture of the Cleveland Public Library, the Junior Council on World Affairs, the *Cleveland Press,* and the Cleveland Museum of Art. Launched in 1945, the program was intended to develop better world citizenship and greater international understanding and deliberately targeted young people "who will reap the most harvest from the years of peace, or pay the greatest penalties in another war" (quoted in Braverman 1979, 155). This program, which continued until 1962, was notable for including students in the planning and implementation of its events—speakers, films, dancers, music, panel discussions, recordings, dramatic presentations, and art exhibits, all designed to introduce attendees to economic, political, and cultural information about different countries. Some observers in Cleveland felt that the program waned in interest and relevance by the end of the 1950s, when education became more oriented to science and overtaking the Russians in space, when television became a more general part of the culture, and when young people became more interested in issues such as dating and grooming.

Much of the club work that was undertaken at the New York Public Library during the Depression years also focused on increasing the civic awareness of young people through discussions and presentations on current events. As noted earlier, the clubs, with their emphasis on programming for teens, became a casualty of post-World War II staffing shortages and a new emphasis on efficiency in library administration.

While doing research for this book, we stumbled on a fascinating pamphlet, *A Youth Library in Every Community,* published by the Young People's Reading Round Table, Division of Libraries for Children and Young People of the American Library Association. It is undated, but the many photos and some internal textual evidence would indicate that it was published in the late 1940s or very early 1950s. It appears to be written for trustees and other civic leaders, giving a rationale for supporting young adult services in their local public libraries. The argument is firmly based on the notion that library services to young adults will help them to help themselves in a time of rapid social change. The first page addresses the reader in one extraordinarily long and complex sentence:

> And now here you are, beset by all the changes that have come along in our pattern of social living,—the rise of industrialism, the growth of cities, the increase of leisure, the menace of bigness,—feeling pretty well buffeted about yourself even though you have a background of stability to enable you to cope with these changes, but mightily concerned with the effect of all these things upon the young people of today, and eager to find ways of helping them to help themselves,—and—AREN'T YOU FORGETTING ONE OF YOUR GREATEST RESOURCES? HAVE YOU THOUGHT OF YOUR PUBLIC LIBRARY?

The rest of this brochure is filled with photos of young people engaged in a variety of activities at their public library: listening to records, watching film programs, participating in panel discussions, putting on programs to promote world understanding, and, of course, reading. Many examples are given of space that libraries had provided for teens, from club rooms to a private home in Sacramento, California, with oriental rugs, coffee tables, a victrola, and a fully equipped kitchen (*Youth Library*, n.d., unpaged).

What is interesting to us looking back at this well-constructed, expensively produced brochure is that the pitch is really based on the civic betterment that could result from investing in young adult library services. The message from the children's and young people's advocates at the American Library Association was that if libraries were properly funded and charged with providing progressive services to teens, those teens would be better able to deal with the social change that seemed to bombard postwar Americans. The message appears to have gone unheeded, however.

Braverman theorizes that young adult librarians, their numbers in decline during the 1950s, turned inward during this period, focusing their attention on their book collections. She acknowledges that the severe staff shortages and heavy staff turnover of the period made it difficult to maintain the kind of proactive services that had been in place earlier. However, she also cites some prevailing social trends that encouraged this passivity in library services to teens. This was the age of conformity, the era of the Man in the Gray Flannel Suit and Senator Joseph McCarthy's paranoid hunt for communists in all areas of American life. Civic engagement other than expressions of basic patriotism was not encouraged. And while public librarians went along with the mainstream of social thought and provided familiar services to patrons much like themselves, the chasm between the mission of the library and the needs of poor, working, and minority young people grew deeper (Braverman 1979, 247ff).

IMPLICATIONS

In retrospect, the 1930s and 1940s look like a golden age in thinking about library services for young adults. It was the one period in which the three pillars of the public library philosophy—reading, education, and the good of the community—all supported the mission of service to teens. Unfortunately, it did not last. Miriam Braverman (1979) observed that specialized public library services for high school students began to wane in the years after World War II. She identified two major reasons for the decline: a shortage of trained young adult librarians to do the work, and an increased emphasis by library managers on scientific management practices that required documentation of workload and evidence of efficiency. Young adult services were staff-intensive and gave more in-depth service to individuals than the more routinized public services such as reference.

The period from 1970 to the early 1990s was not a golden age for young adult services. However, public libraries made some dramatic changes during this time, and these changes would have an impact on more recent and encouraging developments. In the next chapter, we will look at the decades of the 1970s and 1980s as an era of public accountability, in which public libraries turned to business models for new ways to conceptualize and manage their operations. We will try to understand how strategic planning, marketing, and evaluation techniques redefined public library service and laid the groundwork for our next golden age.

CHAPTER 2

We Learn to Think like MBAs

We now come to a period in the development of young adult library services that we experienced ourselves, not as teenagers, but as professionals who participated in the foibles and follies, victories and setbacks, triumph and turmoil of the decades between 1970 and 2000. Our memories are as vivid and occasionally as embarrassing as adolescence itself: a disco contest in the basement of a library in East Los Angeles; an all-day seminar at a suburban library devoted to alternative lifestyles; programs on bicycle repair, songwriting, and underground comics; battles of the bands; the first youth advisory councils; ephebiphobia; the experimental High John library that aimed to institutionalize radical outreach approaches; miniskirts and blue jeans. At times, librarians who continued to serve teens during this period felt besieged, like lonely warriors in a losing battle against institutional indifference, economic pressures, and the professional mainstream.

All around us, public library leaders were learning the vocabulary of management and marketing. Responding to the language and ideas in circulation at all levels of government, they were finding ways to make public libraries accountable to taxpayers who were no longer willing to pay for "nonessential" services. The Public Library Association began to develop planning and evaluation tools that were intended to help local libraries be more credible with taxpayers and policymakers. Meanwhile, at the Baltimore County Public Library, director Charles Robinson was defining a new customer-oriented approach to library service, telling his staff to "give 'em what they want" (*Give 'Em What They Want!* 1992; Rawlinson 1981). Collection development was never the same again. Young adult librarians and other advocates for youth services in libraries, like their colleagues, also found it prudent to begin to think like MBAs.

The three pillars of public library service—reading, information, and community—were still standing, of course. They were inevitably transformed, however, by the new business models that were beginning to dominate our approach to library operations. Considering each pillar in turn will bring us up to the present time and some radical new ideas about ways to connect libraries and teens.

MARKETING BOOKS TO TOUGH CUSTOMERS

Reading continued to be a mainstay of library services, but now librarians were unabashedly and aggressively marketing their wares. Many public libraries looked to the tactics used by successful bookstore chains and began to merchandise their collections with eye-catching stacks of best-sellers at the front entrance and displays of impulse items by the checkout stand.

Young adult areas often lost out in the competition for prime floor space. Where designated teen space still existed, it was often in a remote corner of the library. Creative librarians made the best use they could of the shelves, highlighting the magazines and paperbacks that teens increasingly preferred to bulky hardcover books. They hung posters and other visuals to try to point young customers in the right direction. Ginny remembers making floor pillows to carve out a lounge area in front of the range of shelves allocated for teens at one suburban library and creating a graffiti board on which teens could scrawl their own messages to the world.

Young adult librarians looked back to Margaret Edwards's book talk strategy as another way to market books to teens. Joni Bodart probably did more than any other single individual during this time to make booktalking an essential skill in a young adult librarian's toolkit. Her handbooks made it look easy, and many librarians who had enjoyed telling stories to younger children found booktalking to teens to be just as rewarding. Public librarians looked for opportunities to reach captive audiences of young adults, usually in junior and senior high schools, and ply them with book talks. Did it work? Did the kids read more or better books as a result? We lack the data that would prove it, but many librarians are convinced to this day of the value of this marketing ploy. In fact, we recently heard a leader in the Young Adult Library Services Association (YALSA) claim that booktalking is the most important element in young adult library service. And when the late Michael Printz, much-loved and respected Kansas high school librarian, was asked by Roger Sutton what he did to get kids to read, this was his reply:

> I think the greatest thing for getting kids and books together is the book-talk . . . . there's nothing as great or as powerful as going into a classroom with a cartful of books and talking for twenty minutes about thirty or forty books, then standing out of the way when students come up to get them. Of all the things I've ever done, that would have to be the greatest rush in the world. (Sutton 1993, 155)

YALSA took the lead during this period through two other significant innovations aimed at marketing books and reading to young adults: it instituted awards and prizes for young adult literature, and it established Teen Read Week.

Young Adult Literature Awards

The first major award for young adult literature established by YALSA was named for Margaret A. Edwards, the librarian credited by the association with bringing young adult literature and library services to the attention of the library profession ("Margaret A. Edwards Award" 2002). Established in 1988, it honors an author's lifetime achievement in writing books that are popular with teenagers.

YALSA also honored Margaret Alexander Edwards, called Alex by her friends, with the Alex Awards, first given in 1998. These honors are now awarded annually to the top ten books written for adults that have special appeal to young people between the ages of twelve and eighteen ("Alex Awards: Policies and Procedures" 2002). The awards are sponsored by the Margaret Alexander Edwards Trust and by the ALA review journal, *Booklist*.

Neither the Margaret A. Edwards Award nor the Alex Awards has developed the cachet or prestige associated with the Newbery and Caldecott awards given to distinguished works of children's literature and illustration. The YALSA leadership hopes that its new Michael L. Printz Award will give similar recognition and marketing power to young adult literature. Given for the first time in 2000 to *Monster* by Walter Dean Myers, the Printz Award goes to a book that exemplifies literary excellence in young adult literature. Michael Cart, generally considered the driving force behind the establishment of the Printz Award, said that it "serves notice on the reading, publishing, and bookselling communities that young adult literature has come of age" ("About the Michael L. Printz Award" 2002).

Teen Read Week

On the Teen Read Week website, YALSA credits this activity with stimulating new ideas within its ranks. In particular, the success of Teen Read Week since its inception in 1998 has encouraged the association to focus more strategically on teen literacy, which it defines as "the ability of adolescents to read print materials and to use print materials for many reasons including learning, working, fun, information, knowledge, research, and personal growth" ("Teen Read Week" 2002). This annual event is primarily a public relations venture and is publicized by graphic materials such as posters featuring current icons of teen popular culture.

YALSA has garnered a number of corporate sponsors for Teen Read Week, including New Line Cinema, *Seventeen* magazine, the World Wrestling Federation, and publishers such as Harcourt, Houghton Mifflin, Scholastic, and Random House. Its nonprofit partners include the American Association of School Administrators, the American Booksellers Association, the National Education Association, the National Council of Teachers of English, the International Reading Association, KidsNet, and SmartGirl.org. This annual October hoopla has now come to include considerable media focus on teen reading as well as local activities targeting teens. The number of libraries and teens participating increases each year.

YALSA has also begun promoting summer reading programs for teens, an initiative that is closely related to Teen Read Week in concept. The buzz on electronic discussion lists such as PUBYAC indicates that some young adult librarians are finding this another way to promote books to those tough teen customers. We are indeed indefatigable in our efforts to get those kids reading.

Teens as Readers: What the Research Tells Us

With the increasing focus on book awards, the young adult librarians who comprise the leadership of YALSA have continued to broadcast their belief in the importance of books and reading in the lives of teenagers and as a focus for library services. To their credit, they have also increasingly sought the opinion of teens themselves about the books they choose to market through their Best Book lists. Dedicated young adult librarians have always been able to nurture those few dedicated teen readers who share their own love of books and reading. These are the easy customers to reach, however. What about the majority of teens who do not find reading to be so central to their lives? What do we really know about teens as readers today?

We know that reading assessment scores for teens are not impressive. The 1998 Reading Report Card issued by the National Assessment of Educational Progress was the most recent national assessment of grades eight and twelve. It found that 74 percent of all eighth graders and 77 percent of all twelfth graders were performing at the basic level of reading achievement. That sounds pretty good. However, the results for proficient and advanced levels—the skill levels necessary for coping with complex texts, reading critically, and fully comprehending what is read—were much less encouraging. Only 33 percent of eighth graders and 40 percent of twelfth graders were considered proficient. A mere 3 percent of eighth graders and 6 percent of twelfth graders tested at an advanced level. At all grade levels, girls outperformed boys; and whites outperformed black, Hispanic, and American Indian students. Students eligible for free or reduced-price lunch programs had lower average reading scores than students who were not eligible for the program.

Some of the more nuanced findings of the 1998 study are also interesting. Students at all grade levels who reported talking about their reading with friends or family at least monthly had higher reading scores than students who reported no book discussion of this type. Students in grades eight and twelve indicated less frequent book discussions than they did in 1992. They also reported less television viewing than they had in 1994; there was no indication, however, that they were reading books any more as a result (Donahue et al. 1999). We might speculate that by 1998 teenagers were spending more time in front of computer screens and less time in front of the television screen.

We know that teens who read well are more likely to enjoy reading, and that those who enjoy reading are more likely to read well. In the online survey about teen reading conducted by SmartGirl.org in partnership with the ALA's 2002 Teen Read Week, for example, there was a clear correspondence between those young people who saw themselves as good readers and those who enjoy reading ("Latest Survey Results" 2002).

G. Kylene Beers (1996) has made a special effort to understand aliterate teens—kids who can read but don't. Through a yearlong study of two seventh-grade classrooms, she developed a typology of young adult readers. At the high end, she found a small group of avid readers, young people much like the ones who responded to the SmartGirl survey discussed above. They like to read and make time for it in their busy lives. They identify themselves as readers and have positive feelings about other young people who read. They see reading as "a way of life."

At the other end of the spectrum, Beers identified those young people who are illiterate. They have never learned how to read, which they see as "figuring out words." Interestingly, they may or not see other readers in a negative light; in some cases, they actually admire teens who have mastered this skill that remains elusive for them.

Beers was particularly interested in the largest group of teens, the ones she labeled "aliterate." These are the young people who have mastered the basic skills of literacy but don't read except under pressure. She found three categories of aliterate teens. The dormant readers actually like to read and find it "a neat experience." They identified themselves as readers and have positive feelings about other readers. They just don't have time to read now in this active time of their lives. The second category, "uncommitted" readers, do not enjoy reading and see it as merely a functional skill that they need to use from time to time. They didn't have negative feelings about teens who read; they just didn't put themselves in that category. The unmotivated readers, on the other hand, actually had negative feelings about people who read, calling them "strange" or "boring." They had acquired basic literacy skills but saw little use for them.

We also know that the International Reading Association (IRA) was concerned enough about teen reading to issue a position statement on adolescent literacy in 1999. It is a thoughtful document. The authors observe that adolescents' failure to reach requisite levels of literacy cannot be blamed entirely on teaching or learning failures in their preschool years or in the elementary grades. They point out that teens come to secondary schools with a tremendous range of backgrounds and experiences, including different levels of academic progress. They still need considerable guidance "so that reading and writing develop along with adolescents' ever increasing oral language, thinking ability, and knowledge of the world" (Moore et al. 1999, 4).

The IRA offers seven principles that it believes would support the literacy development of all adolescents. Significantly, these reading specialists, almost all involved with formal education in one way or another, do not claim that schools can do it all. They urge all adults involved in the lives of adolescents to commit themselves to providing teens with programs for literacy development based on the seven principles. While several of the principles refer specifically to pedagogical practices and educational assessment policies, at least two are relevant to public libraries:

- adolescents deserve access to a wide variety of reading material that they can and want to read; and
- adolescents deserve homes, communities, and a nation that will support their efforts to achieve advanced levels of literacy and provide the support necessary for them to succeed.

Certainly, public libraries have made a sea change from the days when young adult collections consisted of row after row of hardcover adult books. Popular teen magazines and paperbacks are now ubiquitous in young adult sections, along with popular music CDs and graphic novels. Whether these materials, presumably "the reading material they can and want to read," will lead to the advanced literacy levels that the IRA envisions for teens is another question, of course.

There is no question, however, that the public library is the community institution most committed to supporting teen literacy, aside from the local mega-bookstore, of course. It is a rare after-school teen program outside of the library that promotes teen reading in any way. Later in this chapter we will talk about the new movement in public libraries to collaborate with community partners. Interestingly, few of these initiatives have focused on connecting teens and books.

We do not know how successful public libraries' efforts to market books and reading to teens have been. Has Teen Read Week, for example, motivated more young adults to read for pleasure or to use the library as a provider for books? We simply do not know. The numbers of participating teens have increased, but this is at least partially due to more libraries participating. Teen Read Week may provide a vehicle for teens who are already readers to reaffirm their commitment to books, and this isn't a bad thing. Teen Read Week might be best understood as a celebration of teen readers, and this is surely a good thing. However, there is still no evidence that it has generated new recruits to the ranks of teen readers. And at least two studies suggest that this kind of pleasure reading ranks low as a library service priority by teens.

Two researchers at the University of South Florida conducted a small study to try to determine what strategies, programs, and services are most effective in attracting young adults to the library (Bishop and Bauer 2002). They gathered data from librarians and from teen library patrons and then compared the results. The only marketing strategy that placed in the top three for both groups was providing refreshments; everybody seems to understand the importance of food to teens. There was more consensus among the librarians and the teens who are already using libraries about what services were most important to them. None of the top three involved pleasure reading. Book discussions, book talks, and author visits ranked low on the list for both librarians and teen library users. Librarians and teens agreed that the Internet, volunteer opportunities, and research were the top priorities in services for young adults. We will discuss the implications of these findings later in this chapter. What is important to understand here is that teens using libraries in at least one state are not particularly interested in learning more about books they might read for pleasure. And the librarians who work with them on a regular basis seem to understand that. They may hang a Teen Read Week poster in the library and do book talks from time to time, but they know that what their teens really want are the resources for doing their school-related research, access to the Internet, and opportunities to volunteer.

The second study was conducted by the Urban Libraries Council. When the council began to administer the Public Libraries as Partners in Youth Development (PLPYD) project for the Wallace–Reader's Digest Fund, it decided to investigate what the potential teen customer of library services really wanted. Using classic marketing strategies, the researchers surveyed young people in a number of communities across the country to see what they said about libraries and their services. They looked for the kids who were not library users. These teens told their interviewers a great many interesting things about their perceptions of the public library. Elaine, who was then the project director for PLPYD, summarized the findings:

- Libraries are not cool; they are frequented by nerds, dorks, and dweebs.
- Library staff are not helpful or friendly.
- Teens need more access to technology and more training in using it.
- Teens want help with their school projects and research.
- Libraries need to provide better books and materials.
- Teens need welcoming spaces—not morgues.
- Library hours of service are not convenient to teens.
- Teens want jobs and volunteer service opportunities.
- Libraries need to get rid of restrictive rules and fees.
- Teens are willing to help libraries become better (Meyers 1999).

Throughout the remainder of this book, we will return to these statements by teens over and over again. What is important to note here is that books and other traditional library materials get only one mention, and that is critical of the quality of libraries' typical holdings. The teens wanted multiple copies of popular books, and they wanted them in good condition. They preferred both the stock and the ambience of a typical Borders or Barnes & Noble store to what they perceived to be the outdated, shopworn goods at their local public library. And clearly, they wanted much more than an appealing book collection.

Some young adult librarians will object; they will point to their own well-chosen, well-maintained collections of popular reading for teens. We just want to point out that even many teens who read for pleasure do not think of the public library as the best place to find books. Whether it is due to fear of fines, discomfort with the quiet, unfriendly environment, or dissatisfaction with the service hours and the collection itself, the public library has not established itself with most teens as a place to go for pleasure reading. Even the young adult readers who took the SmartGirl.org survey mentioned earlier were not frequent public library users; on average, they visited the public library only once every three months.

However effectively the library community goes about marketing books and reading to young adults, these messages are in danger of being submerged in the hype about the Internet and about information. In the 1980s, the public library community began self-consciously to identify its mission with information. Strategic planning became the vehicle for legitimizing information as the appropriate concern of public libraries.

REDEFINING THE PUBLIC LIBRARY AS THE INFORMATION PLACE

Public librarians experienced one of their cyclical crises of purpose in the 1980s. They had gone through the heady days of outreach and service to the underserved in the 1970s, only to find that the rhetoric had gone stale and the funding had dried up when the Democrats left the White House. Taxpayers were in revolt against what they perceived to be exorbitant tax burdens and wasteful government. In California, a well-organized campaign led by an association of landlords resulted in Proposition 13 in 1978, the first of the citizen-generated tax rollback legislation. By dramatically reducing property taxes, Proposition 13 left local governments without the finances to support even mandated services such as public safety, health, and welfare. So-called optional services such as libraries were prime targets for cuts.

Proposition 13 was followed by similar initiatives in other states. An economic recession and a rise in the number of fiscal conservatives elected to office also contributed to a new governmental austerity and a new call for accountability in the management of public services. The ideas in circulation now were an extension of the scientific management principles that had been invoked in the 1950s. Now public administrators, including library directors, would be exhorted to run their organizations like their counterparts in the private sector. Savvy library directors looked for new management techniques. The most compelling of these management tools were strategic planning and systematic evaluation. Through strategic planning, public library directors could presumably direct their leaner resources toward the services most needed or wanted by their customers, formerly known as patrons or users. By using quantitative evaluation techniques, they could document their effectiveness in reaching organizational goals and demonstrate their accountability in the use of public funds.

Strategic Planning and the Expansion of the Public Library's Mission

As early as 1979, the Public Library Association (PLA) was attempting to define a public library mission that would help to communicate the institution's integral place in contemporary society. *The Public Library Mission Statement and Its Imperatives for Service* (Public Library Association 1979) made a case for information services as a basic good that the public library should provide. The venerable Lowell Martin (1983) contributed to the national discussion within the library community by introducing the concept of a menu of roles for the public library, with each local community empowered to make its own choices about service priorities.

The culmination of these efforts, however, was the Public Library Development Project, through which the PLA created two sets of tools designed to enable decision-makers in every public library to do their own planning, role setting, and evaluating. Two manuals—*Planning and Role Setting for Public Libraries* (McClure et al. 1987) and *Output Measures for Public Libraries* (Van House et al. 1987)—were the centerpieces of the new systematic approach to public library accountability. A look at the menu of roles that were offered as options shows us an institution moving away from books and reading toward a more information- and education-oriented emphasis. Here are the eight roles in the 1987 menu, along with their definitions:

- Community Activities Center: The library is a central focus point for community activities, meetings, and services.
- Community Information Center: The library is a clearinghouse for current information on community organizations, issues, and services.
- Formal Education Support Center: The library assists students of all ages in meeting educational objectives established during their formal courses of study.

- Independent Learning Center: The library supports individuals of all ages pursuing a sustained program of learning independent of any educational provider.
- Popular Materials Library: The library features current, high-demand, high-interest materials in a variety of formats for persons of all ages.
- Preschoolers' Door to Learning: The library encourages young children to develop an interest in reading and learning through services for children, and for parents and children together.
- Reference Library: The library actively provides timely, accurate, and useful information for community residents.
- Research Center: The library assists scholars and researchers to conduct in-depth studies, investigate specific areas of knowledge, and create new knowledge (McClure et al. 1987, 28).

Users of the *Planning and Role Setting* manual were reminded that no public library could be all things to all people. Rather, it must think strategically and direct its limited resources to more targeted goals and objectives. Library decision-makers were encouraged to select one primary role and perhaps two to four secondary roles on which to focus their efforts.

The relative lack of attention given to books and reading in this list of possible public library roles is interesting. So is the schizophrenic approach to age levels of service. In both theory and practice, all but one of these roles could conceivably be implemented for all ages. And yet the "Preschoolers' Door to Learning" is limited to children under the age of five. There was concern among children's librarians that literal-minded library directors and trustees would select that role and think that they had adequately addressed the needs of children in their community. Librarians who were active in both the national children's and broader public library communities did their own strategic planning. They succeeded in getting a grant from the U.S. Department of Education (DOE) for a project to develop and field-test quantitative and qualitative evaluative measures for public library services to children that would be related to the planning and evaluation documents already created by the PLA. In the next section of this chapter, we will look more closely at the efforts by children's and young adult librarians to develop evaluation tools.

It is unclear how many public libraries actually implemented the planning and role-setting process. It was supplanted in 1998 by a newer and more complex approach, *Planning for Results* (Himmel and Wilson 1998), which used thirteen service responses, none of which are age-specific, in place of the seven roles. What is important here, however, is that public librarians had jumped on the strategic planning bandwagon, trying to rationalize their services in ways that would demonstrate to elected officials and budget analysts that they were using modern management techniques to guide their operations. The output measures that accompanied the PLA planning and role-setting documents also gave librarians new tools and a new language for proving the effectiveness of their services.

Accountability through Evaluation

The PLA issued its output measures manual simultaneously with the planning and role-setting manual. The message was clear. Good public library directors were expected to be more systematic in their evaluation activities as well as in their planning efforts. By collecting and analyzing quantitative data about their services, they could make better management decisions and provide evidence of accountability to elected officials.

As noted earlier, children's librarians moved first to create evaluation tools specifically for children's services. A joint Association for Library Services to Children/PLA committee hired Ginny to be the principal investigator on the DOE-funded project; she ultimately wrote the new publication that brought children's services into the planning and evaluation picture, *Output Measures for Public Library Service to Children* (Walter 1992). This project, incidentally, was the first time that Elaine and Ginny worked together.

Young adult librarians had a friend in the U.S. Department of Education. Ray Fry, the director of the department's library programs, approached YALSA in 1993, after the children's output measures manual had been published, and asked the association if it would like to produce a similar document for young adult services. He provided the funding, and once again Ginny was pressed into service to write the manual. Once again, Elaine served on the advisory committee. The resulting document, *Output Measures and More* (Walter 1995), has a broader scope than the children's output measures manual. The young adult publication aims to bring teens and their library services into the process from the beginning, starting with planning and ending with evaluating. Throughout the document, librarians are urged to involve teens as participants in the process. There are even output measures to document their participation. Since *Output Measures and More* was based on the eight roles defined by the Public Library Development Project, it continued to highlight the informational and educational services implied by the roles. In a subsequent chapter, we will discuss the continuing need to evaluate young adult services.

Perhaps the most important consequence of the planning and evaluation initiatives for young adult services, however, was that they began to generate data about our customers. The customer focus of both planning and evaluation forced us to listen to them and to hear what *they* found important about the library. When we systematically gathered data about teens in our communities, we learned about other organizations and agencies that provided relevant services. Some of these would become our partners in innovative collaborations. We also learned about glaring gaps in services for young people. We learned where teens spent their time out of school, what they liked about their community, and what worried them. We also learned what they thought about library services. The PLPYD needs assessment project was significant because of its national scope and because of its publication in the library press. Presumably, however, young adult librarians and generalists who advocated for teen library services were following the suggestions in *Output Measures and More* or latching on to other planning activities in their libraries. Some librarians participated in broader planning activities sponsored by local government and were able to bring the library to the youth development table.

In at least some cases, libraries changed their priorities, policies, and practices because of what they learned from their teen customers. Often, what they learned, as pointed out earlier, was that teens wanted homework assistance and access to cutting-edge information technology. We will discuss the public library homework center briefly here and devote an entire chapter to teens and technology and another to evaluation strategies a little later in this book.

Public librarians have often been ambivalent about providing homework assistance. Many have felt that supporting curriculum needs was properly the job of school libraries. Cindy Mediavilla ("Why Library Homework Centers" 2001) has pointed out that when the post-World War II baby boom led to unprecedented numbers of teens coming to public libraries with their homework assignments in the 1960s, many libraries responded by limiting their services to students. Some libraries required teens to produce "library use permits" from parents or teachers; others denied services to students altogether.

Mediavilla found that the public library "blackboard curtain" began to lift in the mid-1980s. Now homework centers exist in public libraries across the country. Teens are involved in these homework assistance programs both as users of the services and sometimes as service providers as well, serving as tutors or technology assistants.

Public library homework centers have a number of implications for young adult services. These programs recognize that teens have a legitimate need for information as a support for their formal learning. The programs position the library as an agency committed to providing important after-school services to young people. Finally, they provide natural opportunities for the library to partner with schools and other youth-serving agencies. These partnerships are an important element in the emerging paradigm of public library services.

COMPETING BY COLLABORATING: A NEW WAY TO THINK ABOUT COMMUNITY

We have chronicled the ongoing efforts by young adult librarians to collaborate with schools, which are certainly the most significant formal institutions in most teens' lives. However, schools are not the only organizations to provide services for young people. Increasingly, librarians are looking for sustainable partnerships with other agencies in their communities that are committed to the healthy development of young people: employment and recreation programs, art centers, churches, and social service centers.

Many of us got our first taste of collaboration in the outreach programs of the 1960s and early 1970s. However, many of the agencies we worked with in those days were funded by short-term soft money. The agencies did not survive, and neither did the partnerships. In fact, competition for scarce funds actually impeded many early collaboration efforts. The negative consequences of this competition for resources have been recognized by many funding agencies as well as by the service providers themselves.

The new approach, therefore, can be characterized as competing by collaborating. The idea is that by collaborating or partnering, two or more organizations with compatible missions can strengthen their competitive edge. Public and nonprofit managers have learned that they must exploit and leverage cooperation for mutual advantage. Management theorists Barry Bozeman and Jeffrey D. Straussman (1990, 51) put it like this: "In the public sector, good strategy is, almost inevitably, multi-organization strategy." They encourage public managers to look for "piggy-back" opportunities that enable them to expand their service domains without reducing their commitment to a core mission. Increasingly, of course, our funding sources are requiring that we document the partners with whom we can collaborate.

Management theorist Rosabeth Moss Kanter (1994) writes about the "collaborative advantage" that effective partnerships provide. She also acknowledges the pitfalls that can occur when two different organizations try to work together, and she suggests strategies for maintaining long-term collaborations. Based on her analysis, we would speculate that most library collaborations we have observed have not achieved the kind of deep integration recommended by Kanter, limiting themselves instead to the development of tactical and operational integration between partners.

It is not easy to build the mutual trust and respect necessary for good partnerships. Nor is it easy to find and commit the time and resources required to make them work. By forging new collaborations, public libraries are nevertheless attempting to increase their capacity and stretch their resources. These partnerships are also changing the way we think about community and the library's place in the community. They are also helping us understand how teens and libraries can work to build community together.

It is important to recognize that community-building has not been at the forefront of public libraries' understanding of their mission. As Kathleen de la Peña McCook (2000) has pointed out, in recent years libraries and librarians have been far more preoccupied with technological change than with issues such as civic renewal, community building, and a revitalized democratic society. With a few exceptions, librarians have not been at the table when policymakers, activists, planners, and theorists have deliberated strategies for building community. And yet it is such an obvious and important role for public libraries to fill.

One of the key findings from the Public Libraries as Partners in Youth Development initiative was that public libraries could—and in many cases, should—become part of what the national evaluation team from the Chapin Hall Center for Children calls a network of community supports for children and youth. The nine libraries involved with the PLPYD project forged partnerships with a wide variety of organizations in their communities: colleges and universities, parks and recreation departments, Head Starts, churches, schools, museums, and other city agencies. It wasn't just the library staff who formed the partnerships, however; the young people themselves were active participants in these collaborations. In Philadelphia, for example, young adult leaders involved with the public library took the initiative to organize an annual Youth Summit that brings together teens from the entire city to learn about education, employment, and personal development opportunities. Where teens are given an opportunity to participate meaningfully in the life of the community, the result is a phenomenon that Karen Pittman, from the For⌐

Investment, has observed over and over again. When
ʒoung people, the young people in return contribute to
ɛm and Pittman 2003). Public libraries can do a great
 of support.

at the heart of the story that Elaine and I want to tell
ᵴ. We will return to it over and over again in the rest
ɪng on, however, we want to talk about one last mar-
ɪn important part of the narrative of young adult
ɛd the twentieth century. This is the marketing of
y community.

O LIBRARIES

ˉ the American Library Association in sweltering
ʏ of us were introduced to a new word: "ephebi-
and loathing of adolescents. Hardy Franklin, the
licated his President's Program to a promotion of
⸺ ɪo youth. The Young Adult Library Services Association sup-
ᵱ⸺ ɪɪs program with the publication of "Beyond Ephebiphobia," a tool
chest to assist librarians recover from lingering cases of ephebiphobia. The tool
chest included a reprint of an article from *Phi Delta Kappan* by Kirk Astroth,
an extension specialist with the Montana state 4-H office. Astroth (1994)
pointed out that the conventional wisdom that most or all teens are at risk is
a misperception that warps the public's attitude toward teens and diverts
attention and resources from the minority of teens who genuinely need help.

This was the opening salvo in a campaign by advocates of library services
for young adults to sell those services to other librarians, particularly their
library directors. And yet the rest of the "Beyond Ephebiphobia" tool chest is
addressed to those who are already young adult advocates, not to those still
presumably in the throes of fear and loathing of adolescence. The tool chest
contains a list of competencies for young adult librarians, prepared by
YALSA. There is a useful guide to gathering information from young people
about library services. There are the usual bibliographies of resources for professionals. It is all strangely inward-looking, claustrophobic, and just a little
defensive. Perhaps its creators felt that they needed to strengthen their supporters before they took their message to the streets, a tactic known to earlier revolutionaries as "consciousness-raising."

A similar tone pervades the training components of YALSA's "Serving the
Underserved" professional development initiative. Serving the Underserved

uses the trainer model to enhance the skills of generalist librarians who interact with teens without having any specialized background. Many of the exercises in the 1996 manual *Serving the Underserved II* seem designed to prevent the rampant spread of ephebiphobia and bring the participants around to a more sympathetic view of teens. Is there an underlying assumption here that teens are underserved in libraries primarily because adults don't like them?

More recent publications from YALSA reflect a movement toward the more positive assets-based language of youth development. However, sometimes when we listen to young adult librarians and advocates for young adult services speak, we hear a more disturbing subtext. The underlying message sounds something like this: "Teenagers are often threatening to adults who do not understand their behavior or their culture. Approaching the reference desk in noisy packs with their last-minute demands for homework materials, they are not preferred library customers. We, the young adult librarians, are really the only people who understand these exotic creatures. However, we need to do more to demystify the tribe of adolescents for our less cool colleagues so they will not undo the good work that we do on behalf of teens."

Of course, we have overstated the tacit message somewhat in order to make a point. But it may be time to tell a different story that would not lend itself to such a negative reading. In the next section of this book, we will tell some counter-stories, narratives that push against both the historical chronicle and the current canon of young adult services.

PART TWO

Rumble Fish

The story we told in part 1 is a familiar one to anybody who has looked closely at library history or spent time in the trenches of public library services for any length of time. It has rarely been pulled together into one coherent narrative, as we have done, but the stories are there for readers and listeners to find.

Part 2 tells some new stories in new voices. Think of these as counter-stories to the traditional narrative of part 1. Look for new themes, new dynamics, and some tensions with the original story. We named this section of the book after S. E. Hinton's *Rumble Fish* because of the way the new voices heard here rumble and sometimes clash like the characters in that novel. We also echo Hinton's theme of insiders and outsiders. The dominant metaphors here, however, are power and empowerment.

Chapter 3 looks at the ways in which principles and practices from the field of youth development can inform a new approach to teen services in libraries, producing the power of partnerships. Chapter 4 confronts teens' fascination with all things digital and discusses the power of technology. In chapter 5, we visit some extraordinary new teen places in public libraries and introduce the power of square footage. Chapter 6 is about listening and the power of teen voices. Finally, chapter 7 reminds us of the power of evaluation as a requisite for accountability and as the missing piece in our advocacy efforts of the past.

CHAPTER 3

Youth Development

The Power of Partnerships

The counter-story of youth development began for Elaine in 1998 when she became director of the Wallace–Reader's Digest Fund's Public Libraries as Partners in Youth Development project. It is a story of libraries learning a new language that gives them a new place and power in their communities. It tells a tale of changes within organizations based on a new understanding of the need to work *with* teens, not just for them. It is a story that leads us to make new promises to teens and gives us tools to keep those promises.

In this chapter we examine youth development as part of human development and attempt to capture the critical and dramatic growth that occurs during the teen years. We also present five premises of youth development and discuss the implications of youth development's challenge to work *with* youth, not just provide services for them. This counter-story illuminates new partnerships between library professionals and teen customers, expands our notion of what being a library professional entails, and situates public libraries as primary supports within their communities.

YOUTH DEVELOPMENT AS PART OF HUMAN DEVELOPMENT

Human development weaves physical, intellectual, emotional, and social development into a holistic web and charts and predicts the work of a lifetime. In the segment of human development defined as youth development, a number of age guidelines exist. One of our favorites is the expression the "second decade," or the "decade of adolescence," a segment between the ages of ten and twenty. Karen Pittman describes this developmental stage as "between the ages of when you don't see them you don't immediately panic because you figure they're okay . . . and when you really wish they would leave home and they haven't" (Meyers, "Youth Development and Libraries," 2002, 256). Pittman suggests that this range might span the ages ten to twenty-two. In fact, economic pressures have forced more and more people to delay their transition to full adult independence until their mid- or late twenties.

Professional library segmentation of this age group has always been messy. Children's rooms and services often provide materials through ages twelve to fourteen as upper limits. The ALA's Young Adult Library Services Association defines its service range as users from twelve to eighteen years. Ultimately, whatever library guidelines recommend is irrelevant to the individual user. The precocious nine-year-old who is determined to read everything Gary Paulsen ever wrote will explore every corner of the library and ask anyone for help. The nineteen-year-old who wants to volunteer during the summer reading program will ask to participate regardless of any age limits we suggest. Positive youth development acknowledges that age limits are very soft at the edges, and that providing opportunities and support for youth during the second decade should be our focus.

Work of the Second Decade

Teens must emerge from the second decade of their lives with the necessary skills to release them from dependence on the support and protection of the family. They must be able to flourish by relying on their own competencies and resources. They are expected to live independently and to be capable of creating and supporting a new family of their own making. They must be able to make a living and to nurture themselves and those who depend on them. Their new role is that of a productive adult member of their society.

To make this transition, youth must grow in five key developmental areas—cognitive, social, emotional, moral, and physical. The National Training Institute for Community Youth Work provides a full look at growth in each of these areas. Based on its framework, we have summarized the key developmental accomplishments of the second decade as:

Youth expand their thinking from concrete to abstract thought.

Youth learn to articulate their own ideas and learn to understand the perspectives of others not like themselves.

Youth learn to plan for the future and are able to construct plans for attaining their goals.

Youth continue to expand their comfort levels with larger social groups—moving from confidence with friends and family into comfort with diverse social settings.

Youth learn to temper strong emotions by developing the ability to take control of situations.

Youth learn coping skills for stress factors such as change, disappointment, or balancing a variety of demands on time and resources.

Young people move from a moral code that has been imposed by family or tradition into an area of personal belief and conviction.

Youth experience a growth spurt equal only to that of their first year of life—typically doubling their weight and increasing their height by 25 percent (National Training Institute 2000, n.p.).

The need for youth to transition from childhood to adulthood is universal and by no means unique to our era or culture. What is increasingly interesting about this developmental phase in our country is the growing discrepancy between the mind and body's ability to perform the work of adulthood and society's willingness to let youth participate in adult duties. The average age of menarche in the United States and other Western countries is now about 12.5 years and has been declining by about 8 months per generation since the start of the twentieth century. Attributed to improved nutrition, this increase in physical maturation exacerbates the gap between physical maturity and the assumption of mature responsibilities. The danger of this gap is that youth feel underutilized and thus undervalued. Jacquelynne Eccles notes that a hallmark of a good community is the "opportunity for youth to matter." Conversely, the lack of this opportunity is a cause for alarm (Meyers, "Youth Development and Libraries," 2002, 257).

The opportunity for teens to make a difference is critical to their development and depends on a system of support from families, adults, and a variety of community organizations. When opportunities to matter are limited, youth can become disengaged. Youth's success in the second decade depends on adults who support them in a twofold manner. First, we must remove barriers that youth face in meeting their developmental goals. Second, we must provide the opportunities and supports for youth to grow. A maxim of youth development is that "problem free is not fully prepared." It is not enough to get out of the way of youth. We must actively engage with them during this critical time of growth.

Librarians have a unique opportunity to provide ways for youth to assume new roles and responsibilities within our organizations. In the

PLPYD initiative, for example, paid and volunteer jobs were created for teens to tutor, offer homework help, assist the public in all areas of technology, create and facilitate programs, serve on advisory councils, and work within the community to help with census workers and clean local parks. Providing youth with opportunities to serve the community and develop skills is not new to libraries. What is new is the powerful support that youth development brings to the work. Our efforts promote a place for youth to matter—to see that they can make a difference. To do this work most effectively, we must understand the process and premises of youth development. This story of process and premises fully develops our understanding of youth development as a coherent approach to facilitating the transition from childhood to adulthood.

YOUTH DEVELOPMENT AS PROCESS: WORKING WITH, NOT FOR

As director of the Public Libraries as Partners in Youth Development project, Elaine's introduction to youth development began with an assignment to interview several young adults and record their answers to three questions. She chose to interview her two teenage neighbors—sisters that she had watched grow up from infancy and knew very well. In spite of her closeness to the girls, she was amazed by their answers to these seemingly simple questions:

1. How do you know an adult cares about you?
2. What are three things teenagers need to succeed at home, at school, and in the neighborhood?
3. What is the most difficult thing about being a teenager?

Since this experience, Elaine has asked librarians around the country to repeat the interview with teens in their communities. They too are genuinely surprised by many of the teens' responses and are touched by the teens' delight in being interviewed. As their interview reports returned, a consensus of teen opinion emerged. Regardless of location or economic status, teens believe:

A caring adult . . .

- provides discipline, safety, and protection
- treats us like an adult by discussing, not commanding
- spends time with us even when they are busy

- meets our needs
- gives us unconditional love.

Success at home, school, and in the neighborhood depends on . . .
- books
- computer access
- transportation
- family support
- will power and mental strength
- trust
- safety and street smarts
- friends
- ability to help others and make a difference.

Difficulties during the teen years include . . .
- knowing what to do when I grow up
- peer pressure
- choices you have to make—"constantly making choices"
- all the changes you go through
- responsibilities
- conflicts with parents.

Our continued delight in reviewing these responses comes with the realization that teens are very aware of the work that they need to accomplish in their second decade. Youth understand that growth depends on a combination of their efforts and supports from family, peers, and community. Teens value and depend on caring adults to work with them in learning the skills needed for adulthood. Teens are not asking that we leave them alone, but to support them during these years of change and challenge. Teens innately understand the premises of youth development, which we will discuss in further detail.

Premise One: Commitment to Youth Participation
The first premise of youth development is that adults must begin to share power with the teens they serve. In the words of the teens we interviewed,

adults need to treat teens "like an adult by discussing, not commanding." The simplest phrasing of this shift in power is to state that librarians need to work *with* teens, not just *for* them.

The goal of youth participation is for youth to develop skills that enable them to become independent of adult supervision and self-sufficient in accomplishing the work at hand. A model for understanding youth participation was developed by the Youth Council of Northern Ireland. We have modified their language to apply to libraries. In this model, youth participation is ranked on a scale from none to the highest level, that of self-managing. The following descriptions define the movement from least to highest youth participation:

None:	Library staff has unchallenged and complete authority.
Tokenism:	Library staff set agendas and make decisions. One or two young people may be consulted, but without the staff necessarily taking heed of their views.
Consultation:	Library staff consult youth, but parameters are set by staff.
Representation:	A select number of young people are put forward as representing their peers, usually via a committee system but with varying degrees of accountability.
Participation:	Youth set agenda, decide on issues and activities, and have joint accountability with library staff.
Self-managing:	Youth manage their group with little or no adult guidance (National Training Institute 2000, n.p.).

While not all youth participation in the library has self-management as a goal, it is essential we understand the full range of participation, and that for youth to become self-managing is the developmental goal of the second-decade work.

It would be inaccurate to say that an understanding of youth participation is new to the public library's vision of young adult services. In 1995, Christy Tyson, writing the introduction to Caroline Caywood's *Youth Participation in School and Public Libraries: It Works,* traced the history of youth participation in library work and emphatically placed it at the heart of successful programs: "young people must have a role in designing the programs that impact them. It isn't enough for young adults to be passive recipients of the services and programs we design for them but, as the only real experts in the needs and interests of young adults, they must be actively involved at a significant and on-going level in program planning, implementation and review." Tyson acknowledged that each library molds its programs based on a number of local considerations, but emphatically concluded that if young people are not "actively involved in setting goals, determining directions and defining activities" the program "will never be truly successful" (Caywood 1995, ix).

In spite of this clear understanding on the part of many library leaders about the primacy of youth participation, participation has not seemed to emerge as the heart of best practice in serving teens. When the first edition of *Excellence in Library Services to Young Adults* was published in 1994, Mary K. Chelton listed the following aspects of young adult services.

Need for separate service for this group:

- guidance to improve reading
- training and level of staff delivering service to young adults
- young adults themselves must participate in the conceptualization and service-delivery process
- young adult specialists are champions for youth, especially in the cultural and social arena

While clearly advocating youth participation, the adult specialists and their skills take priority in this list (Chelton 1994, xi–xiii). A recent book by Patrick Jones, *New Directions for Library Service to Young Adults,* lists twelve goals for a new vision for young adult services (Jones 2002, 11). Of these twelve goals, only one advocates youth participation: "Utilize the experience and expertise of young adults." We believe that the principles of youth development should guide our library processes and that a renewed commitment to active youth participation would reconnect library service with both our community and our teens. Youth participation needs to be at the forefront of our thinking about library services for teens.

Premise Two: Begin with Youth Outcomes

Karen Pittman provides a decade-by-decade tour of youth development in her article, "Balancing the Equation." She documents a movement away from an intervention model begun in the 1960s—an approach to fix what is broken in the lives of troubled teens—toward a prevention model in the 1980s. Prevention models like the "just say 'no' to drugs" or sexual abstinence initiatives asked youth to avoid pitfalls that would hinder their healthy development. The 1990s saw a movement from prevention to a new model based on positive outcomes for youth (Pittman 2000). Pittman suggests that the impetus for this evolution is captured in a bumper sticker motto: "problem free is not fully prepared." We cannot define the work of teens by citing problems they need to have fixed or by listing high-risk behaviors that they have avoided. Instead, we need to develop a list of what teens need to accomplish to enter the adult world fully prepared to succeed and contribute.

In a recent interview, Pittman explains, "the term youth development often is used to define a broader set of outcomes. Especially when we are talking about adolescents and young adults, we need to think about outcomes beyond the negative, the things we don't want youth to do—have sex, use drugs, drop out, join gangs . . . We have to state positive goals as forcefully as we state negative goals about what we want young people to do and not do. We have to have higher expectations" (Meyers, "Youth Development and Libraries," 2002, 256). In the words of the teens from the beginning of this chapter, we need to help teens in their quest to know "what to do when I grow up."

The need to define positive outcomes for youth was addressed by Elaine in creating training materials for the Public Libraries as Partners in Youth Development initiative. These six outcomes are closely based on the 1997 America's Promise Campaign and incorporate the research and action base of the country's leading youth development organizations (Libbey 1999). To succeed in their transition from youth to adulthood, the following youth outcomes are necessary.

- Youth contribute to their community.
- Youth feel safe in their environment.
- Youth have meaningful relationships with adults and peers.
- Youth achieve educational success.
- Youth have marketable skills.
- Youth develop personal and social skills.

It is very interesting to align this outcome list with the information provided by our teen informants in our interviews using the three questions beginning this chapter. Teens told us they needed:

- ability to help others and make a difference
- safety and street smarts; adults to provide safety and protection
- adults to spend time with them and provide discipline and friends and family support

- books, computer access
- to know what to do when I grow up
- will power and mental strength, trust.

While these six outcomes span the work to be accomplished, we recommend that you explore the outcomes desired for the youth in your community and adopt local outcomes when possible. We have seen libraries contribute in some way to all of the positive outcomes, but you may want to focus on two or three that are particularly needed by the teens in your community. Examples of programs that provide outcomes are state education systems, local youth initiatives such as Robert Woods Johnson's SAFE and SOUND initiatives, and municipal offices of youth and education.

Premise Three: Asset-Based Approach

The need for an asset-based foundation for all youth development is most effectively expressed in the work of Northwestern University's Asset-Based Community Development (ABCD) Institute. Under the leadership of John P. Kretzmann and John L. McKnight, the institute works to build communities "from the inside out" by finding and mobilizing the assets within the community.

Kretzmann and McKnight capture their core message using the image of a half-filled glass. Holding the glass before the audience, they ask you to think of the glass as a teen—saying that you have a choice in describing the individual. If one thought of what was missing in the glass (deficit model), one might say that "Marie is an at-risk pregnant school dropout." If one looked at what was in the glass (asset model), Marie would be described as "a star in the church choir and excellent actress in the school play." The choice we make in working with assets or fixing deficits determines our success and the sustainability of our intervention with our teen communities.

Kretzmann and McKnight believe that sustainable change can only occur when programs build on the capacities that exist within the community and within youth. The task of both youth and community development is to "identify capacities and connect them to people, groups and places that can use these capacities." The ABCD Institute provides a list of assets that apply to most teens:

- time
- ideas and creativity
- connection to place
- dreams and desires

- peer group relationships
- family relationships
- credibility as teachers
- enthusiasm and energy (Kretzmann and McKnight 1993, 30–31).

It is important to mention the work of the Search Institute's "Forty Developmental Assets" and distinguish this valuable work from our broader use of the term "asset" as a philosophy and approach to developing teen services and programs. Search provides a framework that "identifies forty critical factors for young people's growth and development. When drawn together, the assets offer a set of benchmarks for positive child and development" (Search Institute). Knowledge of the Search Institute's unique framework for assessing the developmental health of youth and communities is essential and especially valuable if your community subscribes to this approach and measurement method.

Premise Four: Youth and Community Development

Leaders in youth development anchor their work within the community, agreeing with Karen Pittman that youth grow up in communities, not in programs. Pittman explains youth development as "Young people and adults working to create the necessary conditions for the successful development of themselves, their peers, families and communities" (Pittman 2000, figure 2). The Carnegie Foundation's Michele Cahill reminds us that "Communities are dependent upon the minds, hearts and hands of their young people and youth are dependent upon the viability, vitality, protection and attention of their community" (Cahill 1997, 1). The vitality of the library as a community institution is integral to a discussion of youth development. The Chapin Hall Center for Children at the University of Chicago affirms that teens thrive "in communities that link families, government services, and private and community organizations into a web of supports" (Whalen and Costello 2002, 4). The role of the public library in a web of community supports for youth is at the heart of our fourth premise.

The Chapin Hall Center for Children maintains that healthy communities are ones that provide a web of support for youth. If one envisions a web, the strength comes from each juncture or knot in the web. Chapin Hall refers to these points of strength as *primary supports*. Communities rely on a web of primary support organizations if youth are to flourish. Libraries can recognize themselves in the following description of a primary support organization: "they are voluntary, socially inclusive, and developmentally appropriate" (Costello et al. 2000, 1). Primary supports are rooted in the community, and "their ways of relating to children and parents . . . can build individual capacities, help compensate for changes in families and other institutions, provide natural sources of help, . . . and increase the effectiveness of specialized services" (Wynn et al. 1994, 7).

One of the greatest community assets of the public library is its voluntary and socially inclusive structure. Karen Pittman contrasts the social structures of schools and libraries: "Schools are places where young people have limited choices in how they are grouped and what they learn. Libraries . . . are places where young people can actually find their own groupings and choose what they want to learn" (Meyers, "Youth Development and Libraries," 2002, 258). Primary support organizations compensate for changes in families and other institutions. As some schools are pressured to teach toward standardized tests, libraries will continue to serve the independent learner. Libraries can provide safe places and enriched activities to fill the non-school hours as parents are drawn away from home and into the workplace.

As information places, libraries will continue to increase the effectiveness of specialized services by offering community referrals and bringing community groups together on neutral turf to have conversations about the community good. The library as a forum for discussion has special significance for our teen customers as well as the adults who serve and work with them. Our ability to bring together other primary support organizations to discuss our effectiveness with teens in our community is another natural function of libraries. Our ability to partner with community organizations enables us to provide programs and training for teen workers and library staff and increases our many links with our communities.

Primary supports must also be developmentally appropriate, and we look to youth development to help us understand how libraries must change if they are to become developmentally appropriate for teens. Our ability to discuss and embrace the premises inherent in youth development will assure our success as a primary support organization. The power of knowing the language and principles of youth development is the first essential step for libraries to connect in new ways to their communities.

Premise Five: Programs Have Duration and Intensity

One of the most provocative discussions for many of the PLPYD project directors occurred when they were asked to create program plans that responded to information gathered from teens during the first data-gathering and planning year of the initiative. The Wallace–Reader's Digest Fund program officer Catherine Pino worked intensely with project staff to understand a new way of envisioning programs. Elaine captured this new definition of "program" as follows:

> an organized series of challenging supports and opportunities of sufficient intensity and duration to provide significant benefits to participating youth. Programs begin with a desired outcome for youth and then develop activities and opportunities to achieve these outcomes.

The challenge of distinguishing a single event that the library had previously called a "program" (a poetry slam, for example) from the expanded program definition was overcome by additional training and experience. Some of the most helpful training came from the Academy for Educational Development, which defined and distinguished supports from opportunities as:

1. *Supports:* Things done *with* the young person—interpersonal relationships addressed by expectation, guidance, and boundaries
2. *Opportunities:* Activities, roles, and responsibilities taken on and done *by* the young person—chances to explore, express, earn, belong, and influence (National Training Institute 2000, n.p.)

The heart of planning a program incorporates all the premises of youth development discussed so far. An understanding of the range of youth participations from tokenism to full responsibility enables program planners to distinguish between supports and opportunities and to include both in program plans. The ability to define outcomes for youth is the heart of the program plan. Identifying and using youth assets help to inform program plans, and the use of community resources completes a sound youth development program.

The Free Library of Philadelphia's Youth Empowerment Summit serves as an excellent case study of the new program model. In the course of the PLPYD initiative, the Free Library hosted three youth summits, each progressively building on a deepening understanding of youth development. The first summit was envisioned by library staff as a daylong retreat to provide Philly teens with needed information and opportunities to network with each other and with library and community staff. While all agreed that the objectives of the summit were worthwhile, as library staff became more steeped in the premises of youth development, their program process changed. Beginning with the second year of the initiative, teens and staff began with the outcomes for youth participants and then constructed the program model with specific opportunities and supports needed to assure these positive outcomes. The library determined that youth would contribute to their community, learn and demonstrate leadership skills, develop program management skills, and have positive social interactions with peers and community adults for the second year of the summit. Community partners and library staff were enlisted to provide training in marketing, videography, leadership development, and program management. In the third year of the summit, the same program design was used, but teens increasingly assumed full leadership responsibility for program content, training of new teens, community contacts, menus, design of T-shirts and print materials, and publicity.

IMPLICATIONS

Youth development asks libraries to consider a new role as a primary support institution within their communities. This role acknowledges the strengths of libraries as neutral, safe public spaces and inquires how staff can support youth and provide new opportunities for them to grow and contribute to their community. Libraries are asked to be intentional in the use of their resources and to work with the community toward the achievement of developmentally appropriate outcomes for youth. The range of possibilities for libraries to succeed in this role is endless, and we will explore it more fully in the last part of this book.

The next chapter tells a story that teens find particularly compelling. It is the story of empowerment through technology.

CHAPTER 4

Citizens of the Digital Nation
The Power of Technology

When Walt Crawford and Michael Gorman told the story of libraries and technology in 1995 in their book *Future Libraries,* the subtitle was *Dreams, Madness, and Reality.* Their book was a much-needed corrective to a prevailing story they characterized as librarians overcome by "technolust." The counter-story we want to tell about teens, technology, and libraries has a different theme. In our story, the protagonists are not librarians but rather the young people who have claimed technology as their own. Playing supportive roles in our story are the librarians and library workers with new job titles—technology specialists, digital resource managers, homework helpers—who are trying to harness the power of technology to help teens achieve important developmental outcomes.

A fifty-something friend of ours recently reported that she had finally acquired a cell phone. She called her twenty-something son to brag about this leap into the brave new world of telecommunications, and he replied, "Welcome to the 1990s, mom." We suspect that few of us who are old enough to be veteran library professionals will ever catch up to the sons and daughters, the young adults who can truly be called citizens of a digital nation. The teens we want to attract to our libraries think about and use digital technology much differently from the ways in which most of us adults do. This is an area in which most of are still "so last century."

Technology has certainly transformed our libraries. Public Internet access is available at almost every public library, even the smallest and most rural. With the help of Gates Foundation grants and the support of local government, public libraries are wired and equipped with banks of personal computers. Well-funded libraries make a valiant effort to keep their hardware and software up-to-date. Teens expect to see computers in libraries, and librarians expect to see teens using the computers. Don Tapscott (1998) points out that teens have grown up with computers; the machines have always been there, in their classrooms and in many of their homes. He claims that computers have transformed the way young people learn, play, and interact with each other. But what are they doing as they cluster in front of the monitors in our public libraries?

PROVIDING INFORMATION THROUGH THE INTERNET

Yes, many young adults are looking for information on the Internet, especially if they are doing their homework. A recent study funded by the Pew Charitable Trust found that at least 78 percent of all young people between the ages of twelve and seventeen go online for school or personal use. An astonishing 94 percent of these online teens report that they prefer to use the Internet over all other sources for school research. Some of those teens confess to using the World Wide Web as a shortcut, allowing them to minimize their efforts or even to cheat by plagiarizing material. Others found that the Internet enabled them to collaborate on projects across time and distance (Levin and Arafeh 2002).

The number of homes with computers and Internet access has grown so rapidly that we hesitate to cite current numbers. Households with school-age children are particularly likely to report computer ownership. However, the students themselves are concerned about the Digital Divide, according to the Pew study cited above. Ginny and Cindy Mediavilla have also found in their evaluation studies of public library homework centers that young people cannot rely on home computers for school assignments. Even young people who have a computer at home often find that it is inadequate for their purposes. The Internet access may be slow or the word-processing software outdated. They complain about competition from other siblings for the family computer. They also welcome the assistance they get from trained homework helpers at the library.

The ease with which young adults turn to computers for homework sources has led many adults to believe that they are competent, effective users of digital information. The research does not support this belief, however. While teens are comfortable with computers, they are surprisingly naive information searchers. Dania Bilal's research with seventh graders, for example, showed that these students tended to rely on looped searches and hyperlinks. When search tasks were complex and required critical thinking to determine the relevance of information and to construct new meaning from resources, they were less successful. These young teens lacked the information literacy and research skills that could help them make the link between what they already knew and what they needed to discover (Bilal 2000; Bilal 2001).

Another study of the web-searching behavior of high school students produced an interesting metaphor: "Searching the World Wide Web is like visiting a shopping mall the size of Seattle" (Fidel et al. 1999, 24). The teens in this study had all used the Internet but had never received any formal training in searching strategies. They were surprisingly naive about the information available on the Internet. Many thought it had been placed there by one mammoth clearinghouse, probably Microsoft. They were unaware of search engines, evaluation criteria, or search strategies, relying instead on past experience and the assistance of their peers to locate new information. And yet, like the teens in the Pew study mentioned earlier, they preferred the Internet to the library's print resources as a source of information for homework; they liked its immediacy, convenience, and interactivity.

Some public libraries have begun to provide homework helpers: technologically savvy peers or adults who can mediate between teens' need for information, their preference for digital media, and their lack of information literacy skills (Mediavilla, *Creating the Full-Service Homework Center,* 2001). Some of the PLPYD project sites found that technology was an irresistible lure to many teens. At the King County (Wash.) Public Library, for example, young adults were given training and became a cadre of TechnoTeens who were empowered—and paid—to assist library patrons to use computers more effectively. Technology is also a key element in the effective leadership development program that is an ongoing element of youth services at the Free Library of Philadelphia.

The Santa Monica Public Library used Library Services and Technology Act funds and support from the city government to provide teens with extensive training in the use of the library's digital resources and then paid them to work with the public as "information navigators." Ginny evaluated the project for the library and discovered that the teens' information literacy skills and their knowledge of the library's resources did improve somewhat as a result of the training they received. What was most surprising to her, however, was the unusually high satisfaction levels that patrons reported from their interactions with the teens. On feedback forms, the patrons volunteered comments such as "very competent and gracious" (Walter 1999).

Librarians tend to look with some favor on teens' use of technology as a source of information. This is a fairly comfortable and logical extension of our traditional information services, after all, and it does indeed support the development of young adults' academic and job-related skills. However, Linda Braun (2002) reminds us that teens only use digital resources for technology when they must. What they really want to do with computers is communicate.

FACILITATING COMMUNICATION

Ginny gets frequent e-mail messages from her eleven-year-old granddaughter. She lives only half a mile away, and they see each other regularly; but Viv loves to send Internet greeting cards and the virtual equivalent of the chain letters that intrigued her grandmother nearly fifty years ago. She likes to sprinkle her messages with emoticons and excels at the breezy conversational style and informal punctuation and spelling that typify her generation's Internet communications. This young teenager lobbies her parents relentlessly for a computer and phone line of her own and moans about the limitations placed on her time online. Overwhelmingly, what she is doing online is interacting nonstop with friends and, occasionally, with doting adult relatives.

Before the Pew Charitable Trust funded the study on young adults' use of the Internet for homework, it looked at how teens use the Internet to communicate. What it learned was that teens' favorite Internet pastimes are e-mail, chat, and instant messaging. This online revolution in communication has profound impacts on the way that teens maintain friendships and family relationships (Lenhart, Rainie, and Lewis 2001). If teens find it difficult (or too much trouble) to master the skills of information searching on the Internet, they nevertheless seem to find it very easy to connect online with other people.

Teens have found that the Internet not only facilitates communication with friends and family: it also gives them a broader voice. Through electronic discussion lists and chat rooms, they can speak and listen to a far more diverse community than they can in their own geographical neighborhoods. Eliza Dresang writes about young people in the United States communicating with their counterparts in Kobe, Japan, after the 1995 earthquake, and about young Chechens using the Internet to contact Americans during the violent unrest in that region. Gay and lesbian teens have found a safe haven on the Internet that eludes many of them in their own homes and schools (Dresang 1999, 68ff).

Linda Braun (2002) challenges librarians to be more proactive about responding to teens' nearly insatiable desire to keep in touch. She urges them to take the time and trouble to integrate communication functions with more traditional information services on their libraries' computers. Teens will respond, and they will reap positive developmental outcomes along the way.

FOSTERING CREATIVITY

At libraries where technology and teens coexist most happily, we have observed an interesting phenomenon. Teens are not passive users of technology; they use it actively. For many teens, digital technology is a medium for creativity.

Teens have used digital technology in public libraries to produce newsletters and posters, streaming webcasts, and remarkable home pages. Given the requisite tools, training, and encouragement, teens respond to the creative promise of technology. Kids have used digital cameras to document life in their neighborhood and then share it with other young people a continent or more away. Of course, schools sometimes provide these opportunities. Public libraries, however, are in the unique position of being able to uncouple the technology from the curriculum. In a public library, teens can unleash their creativity and let it soar where it will.

Teens have also discovered the power of play on the Internet. While girls are drawn to the communication features, many boys are mesmerized by the games. While the violent and racist nature of many popular computer games has been justifiably criticized by many, there is also much that is creative and positive about digital play. The interactivity of games like the commercial product SimCity or the online NeoPets website allows kids to participate in the creation of virtual worlds. This is valuable role play for big kids who would no longer feel comfortable with the imaginative games of their childhood.

POLICY ISSUES: ETHICS, RIGHTS, AND RESPONSIBILITIES

While librarians tend to fret over the financial aspects of computers and the hassle of managing hordes of sometimes unsavory Internet users, we suspect that the thornier concerns are those involving ethical, legal, and policy issues. These are particularly compelling when the Internet users are teens.

We begin with the assumption that both young adults and librarians have rights and responsibilities when it comes to dealing with what some people have called the "dark side" of the Internet.

Jon Katz, a regular contributor to *Wired* magazine, has come up with a useful framework for thinking about kids and the Internet. He bases it on a vision of the responsible child. The responsible child—or teen—works well in school, has demonstrated that he or she does not intend to hurt others, carries a reasonable share of work at home, and avoids drugs, alcohol, and cigarettes. Katz argued that such children have earned the right to be respected, along with some additional significant rights: to help define literacy, education, and civics for their generation; to have unrestricted access to their culture; to assemble online; and to have equal access to new technologies that deliver information, education, and culture. He argues that using blocking devices such as software filters or V chips is an abuse of adult power. This abuse erodes trust and rational discourse between adults and young people. He points out the obvious problem that filters don't work. More seriously, however, he speculates, "Some children reared on this stuff will inevitably grow up thinking that the way to deal with topics we don't like is to block them—remove them from our vision and consciousness" (Katz 1996, 170). Like many of us in the library profession, Katz believes that parents have the responsibility to guide their children personally into cyberspace, helping them understand what is inappropriate or dangerous.

It would be difficult to implement a policy based on Katz's vision of the responsible child in the public library. We have no way of knowing whether the young people sitting at our computer workstations carry their weight with household chores or experiment with cigarettes. We also do not ordinarily curtail anybody's intellectual freedom based on such standards. However, we could work with the young people in our libraries to define responsible library and Internet behavior and develop acceptable use policies accordingly. We were impressed with the seriousness with which teens approached the task of developing a Library Teen Bill of Rights (see chapter 6). They are sometimes more conservative in their approach to rights and freedoms than adults are. They know where their individual freedoms stop and parental or adult responsibilities begin.

At the very least, teens have the right to prove themselves responsible Internet users. It is only fair that they be given access to the skills and knowledge to do so. Librarians can ensure that young adults know the rules of the road—not just the information literacy skills that will make them more effective and efficient Internet users, but also the rules for civility and privacy that will make them competent citizens in the digital nation. We like the way Frances Jacobson, the librarian at the lab school at the University of Illinois at Urbana–Champaign, has taken the responsibility to teach high school students the basics of netiquette as well as the fine points of information literacy (Jacobson and Ignacio 1997).

IMPLICATIONS

Much earlier in the dawning of the digital age, Ginny wrote about the policy implications of technology for youth services librarians (Walter 1997). She concluded that article by constructing a children's digital library policy meta-narrative. Using a method much like the one we have devised for this book, she untangled the strands of narrative that made up the story. There was a subplot about the efforts of crusading adults determined to protect innocent children and youth from sexual cyberpredators. There was a whole story cycle about the young technogeek surfing the Web with ease, if not grace. There were earnest story lines about the worker of the future, diligently acquiring job skills for the twenty-first century, and about the digital scholar enjoying the resources of a library without walls. She noted that the differences in these stories lay in their varying construction of the image of the child.

The policy metanarrative that Ginny finally told was based on developing a positive relationship between the computer and the young person. Librarians and other adults would play minor roles; kids and their machines would take center stage. She pointed out that it would be an episodic story, proceeding in fits and starts to no foreseeable end, more like a "choose your own adventure" narrative than a fairy tale with a "happily ever after" ending.

This story, first told in 1997, still resonates for us in 2003. We think it is the story young people themselves would tell if asked to write the teens, technology, and library narrative.

CHAPTER 5

Teen Places

The Power of Square Footage

The counter-story of teen places begins in the Los Angeles Public Library (LAPL) in the early 1990s. The tale opens in the bleak landscape of California's Proposition 13, and lead roles are played by the California State Library, library teen councils, and numerous leaders in the Los Angeles Public Library. The star of the story is Teen'Scape, the groundbreaking teen place first opened in 1994 and expanded in 2000. Teen'Scape offers a "CyberZone" with nineteen Internet-access computers; a Living Room with television, film, and comfortable furniture; a Lounge zone for informal socializing and independent reading; group study rooms; and extensive reference and popular collections in a variety of formats. The theme of the story is one of vision and groundbreaking courage and commitment to teens.

Waiting in the wings are staff from the Phoenix Public Library who want to write the next chapter of the story and create a teen place of their own. They are encouraged to take the best of Teen'Scape, learn from the LAPL's experience, and build an even better place. Phoenix staff adopt the principles of youth development and engage teens in a dynamic planning process for the new teen place. Teen Central opens in April 2001 and the world literally comes to see this new place. Among the visitors are staff from the Public Libraries as Partners in Youth Development sites who can no longer ignore the insistent voice of teens from their communities clamoring for places of their own. The power of this story springs from the historic readiness of libraries to listen and a library culture willing to change its concepts about public space.

As Ginny suggests in our first chapter, Andrew Carnegie's provision of designated children's rooms contributed to the institutionalization of public library service for children. Once a place for children was provided, innovative librarians applied their knowledge of child development and of best practices and materials to create child-friendly environments. Children's rooms and children's services have been sustained in public libraries ever since.

Designated places were hallmarks of the first golden age of teen services as well. The early architects of teen services jumped at the chance to convert existing buildings, meeting rooms, or other public areas into places where teens could socialize, play games, conduct programs, have public discussions, and hold club meetings, as well as read and meet their formal and independent educational goals. They understood that place was essential for service. They were not tentative and did not settle for small corners with a few books and posters on the wall. They knew that place conveyed importance and permanence.

Our discussion in this chapter is not centered on how to create teen places so much as on how to think about place. As the language of youth development provided a new vocabulary for discussing library roles, we have chosen the language of an American architect to frame our discussion of place. The ideas and language of architect W. G. Clark suggest a three-part approach to place—a physical place, cultural place, and spiritual space. We especially agree with Clark's assertion that the very act of providing a place affirms the necessity of the place. "In settlement, we are only comforted when we see evidence of the necessity to occupy . . . it is not necessary that buildings be beautiful, but it is necessary that they be necessary" (Jensen 2000, 11). Clark's framework captures the critical message of place and affirms what teens have known intuitively about our public libraries. The power of place lies squarely in the landscape and the necessity of teens to inhabit a place of their own within our libraries.

Teens understand that place conveys both necessity and acceptance. A key finding of the PLPYD planning year was a consensus among teens that the library has no welcoming place for them. Typical of focus groups around the country, teens in Charlotte, North Carolina, recommended that the library needed to develop "a place for kids just to hang out" and conduct their own activities. Conversely, when teens are provided appropriate place, they respond with appreciation and enthusiasm. Here is the reaction of Angela Connell, the president of the Burton Barr Central Library Teen Council in Phoenix, to the city's new Teen Central: "The Teen Central is a dream come true. It is not just a room. It is a haven; a club, a place just for the younger generation to learn, hang out and be sheltered. The room has impacted me in so many ways" ("Highsmith Award Description" 2002, 1). As the three pillars of reading, information, and community enable us to see the whole of library service, Clark's three aspects of place allow a full exploration of library teen places.

W. G. CLARK'S VIEW OF PLACE

W. G. Clark is an AIA award-winning architect who began his career in Charleston, South Carolina, and formed the firm of Clark and Menefee Architects and later Clark Architects. Elaine was first introduced to Clark by Richard Jensen, one of the architects of the Phoenix Public Library's Teen Central. Jensen's book, *Clark and Menefee,* features excerpts from the writings of Clark. This was our introduction to the distinction between space and place. This distinction transformed our planned chapter on library spaces into a discussion of place. While thinking of spaces conveyed a sense of area and even of design, thinking of place as defined by Clark truly expanded our discussion and provided an illuminating framework for this chapter. The richness of place is captured thus by Clark:

> Every site contains three places: the physical place with its earth, sun-light, and view; a cultural place, the locus of the traditions of human intervention; and a spiritual place, or that which we would call an evocative presence, which stirs our imaginations and send us in search of images, memories and analogues. These three aspects of place roughly correspond to body, mind, and spirit. (Jensen 2000, 13)

Interestingly, when Elaine reviewed teen comments from focus groups, teens use "place" rather than "space" consistently in their discussion of needed areas in public libraries.

Clark's construct invites us to find the right physical terrain, whether in an existing or new library building. It invites us to explore the cultures of library teen spaces and acknowledges that we must understand both library culture and teen culture in order to create authentic place. The last and most challenging discussion in this chapter centers on the spiritual or evocative nature of place. We will consider what stirs the teenage imagination and evokes a connection to the community and the larger world.

Physical Place

Physical place within a library is not measured merely in square footage and shaped by its edges. The quality of place is impacted by its light, the views within the space, and the materials used in construction. Planning physical place requires that we ask what area is available and needed to adequately serve the teen population. We need to listen to teens as they provide direction on the views that give them pleasure and areas to avoid when placing teen rooms. Lastly, we need to survey the landscape of the library and determine what edges will contain the proposed teen areas and how new teen places will work in harmony with the existing library terrain.

ADEQUATE SIZE

The size of a teen place is a major consideration and depends on many factors. In searching for a standard for square foot per capita, Elaine discovered a surprising reluctance to discuss size in American public libraries. The U.S. Federal-State Cooperative Service does not include square footage per capita data ("Hennen's American Public Library Ratings" 2002, FAQ). The "Ontario (Can.) Public Library Guidelines" propose a user space required as "30 square feet per user space @ 5 user spaces per 1,000 population" ("Ontario Public Library Guidelines" 1999, 26). A new rating index in Germany, "BIX—The Library Index," will measure "square meters accessible to the public per 1,000 inhabitants" ("BIX" 2001, 3), but there is no consistent formula to help in computing a recommended range for square footage based on population.

The lack of a formal standard for computing square footage for public library buildings doesn't mean that size isn't important. In fact, the lack of a standard often leads to a lively debate on the proper allocation of space. The value of assigning square footage to a population or service conveys commitment and worth. An informal conversation between two library directors confirms this value. One director proudly proclaimed that she was planning to build the largest young adult space in the country and quoted a planned square footage of 11,000. Without a moment's hesitation, the second director countered, "Well, we're planning a space in our renovation—it will be 11,002 square feet." While these remarks were made in jest and the spirit of healthy competition, they do say a world about the message of worth inherent in square foot allocation.

Benchmarks for space allocation can be found in a study of recently planned or constructed teen places in public libraries. Using the total square footage of the library and the actual footprint of the teen space, Elaine created a grid that reflects the gross percentage of space allocated for teens. (See figure 5-1.) The square foot allocation for teens varies between 1 and 5 percent of total square foot allocation. While this seems a small amount, it serves as a starting point for a discussion of what is really needed by a community.

FIGURE 5-1 Square foot allocation for teen places in public libraries

Library	Library square feet	Teen square feet	Percentage of total library space
Orrville Public Library	25,000	612	2
King County Burien	20,000	425	2
King County Lake Hills	9,100	425	5
Burton Barr Central Library	280,000	5,000	2
Ironwood Public Library	15,000	288	2
Mesquite Public Library	20,000	720	4
Cesar Chavez Public Library	25,000	750	3
Juniper Public Library	14,435	150	1
Desert Sage Public Library (proposed)	13,400	576	4
Desert View Public Library (proposed)	15,000	576	4
Cholla Public Library	35,000	600	2
Los Angeles Public Library Teen'Scape	538,000	4,333	1

Regardless of its size, a space must be well used to be successful. Some of the most successful of our new teen spaces report foot traffic and usage of staggering proportions. Since its opening in April 2001, the Phoenix Public Library's Teen Central continues to record 300–500 teens a day using the 5,000-square-foot facility. In a recent conversation with King County Library System administrator Bruce Adams, Elaine asked about the use of their new teens' places. Bruce replied, "They're hopping. Very well used." We encourage planners to study use patterns and demographics to build a strong case for providing the most square footage available and not to rely on past tradition to guide the decision. Teens have told us that if we build it well, they will come and return with their friends again and again.

FOUND SPACES

One strategy for finding space in existing buildings is the identification of areas where library use patterns have changed. Technology has transformed the use of many services within public libraries. Online periodicals have diminished the use of once-flourishing newspaper and magazine rooms. The Long Beach Public Library recently converted those old newspaper and magazine rooms in its branches to family learning centers. Digitization allows genealogical information and special collections to be accessed from home, and many special collections require less storage and public space.

Special music or audiovisual rooms are underutilized, since patrons can now access a wide range of audio and video from the Internet. A simple analysis of circulation and door-counts at many libraries reveals that teens are using collections and services at a much higher rate than readers of adult fiction within a similar space. Examples of underutilized spaces recently converted to teen areas include the following ones.

- A 5,000-square-foot planned but unfunded music room at the Phoenix Public Library's Burton Barr Central Library was converted to Teen Central.

- Some 3,000 square feet from the second-floor periodicals section at the Oakland Public Library Main Building were used to create the planned TeenZone Department.

- An underutilized educational resource area at the Tucson Pima Public Library was converted to the 1,000-square-foot Main Library Teen Resource Center.

- Space was reallocated in King County Library System buildings—primarily from adult periodical and fiction areas—to create new 425-square-foot Teen Zones.

In the foregoing examples, Tucson and Phoenix found space in self-contained existing rooms—the easiest found space to work with, since the place has already been defined in the library landscape. Oakland and the King County Library System had the more common experience of finding underutilized space within an existing area. Teen places need to be self-contained, and the challenge of creating edges for found or newly planned spaces opens our next discussion of physical place.

LANDSCAPE AND EDGES

W. G. Clark observes that "good cities have distinct edges, whether natural of designed" (Jensen 2000, 12). The distinction between natural and designed edges again allows us to think in new ways about physical place. While

Clark's reference obviously refers to land, and natural edges would constitute lakes, rivers, mountains, etc., we are defining natural edges within the library landscape as those that cannot be modified and are integral to the whole of the building. Designed edges are those created by architects to confine designated areas. We will look at several examples of edges that are desirable and those that are not.

Just as natural edges on land become the most desirable locations—lake view properties or mountain foothills, for example—natural edges within buildings are also premium locations. Natural edges in libraries are permanent and include exterior walls and windows. Interior natural edges also include architectural elements that are integral to the total design such as balconies, atriums, and, for our discussion, historically protected features.

Of these natural edges, teens gravitate toward an edge with a view or access to the outside. Phoenix teens recommended an area with an outside patio, with trees, benches, fountains, and relaxing music. While these natural edges are preferred by teens, they are also highly desirable to all library customers—comparable to the corporate "corner office." Happily, a number of newly created teen areas have designated these natural vistas as edges for teen places. The Houston Central Library's ConnecTeens space takes advantage of large windows, and all of the teen places in the Phoenix Public Library look out on wonderful exterior views. Teens are not unique in responding to light and exterior vistas, and they realize the value conveyed by assigning these premium natural edges to their teen places. The wonder of these views is that they provide vistas from within and without. While teens enjoy the view of their city or town, people looking through the glass from the outside can clearly see the teen place in use and know that teens are welcome.

The challenges of historically preserved spaces as immovable or natural edges have been faced by two urban libraries in their recent creation of teen places. When the Los Angeles Public Library and the Brooklyn Public Library began to plan for teen spaces, they were both working within historic buildings with stringent preservation guidelines. In the case of the Los Angeles building, its natural edges, while beautifully preserved, were not the best "view" for the city's trendier teens. The solution was to create new edges within the space by creating a fabric tent ceiling and walls within walls. The Brooklyn Public Library solved the limits of its historic landscape by creating a 1,200-square-foot technology loft—creating new edges above the existing ones. Creative solutions abound for natural edges that at first glance may seem restrictive.

While natural edges present opportunities and challenges, it is the designed edges within our landscapes that are the most prevalent and often define teen places. The location of designed edges is more flexible within buildings, but a few rules of thumb should be mentioned. When Phoenix teens were interviewed and asked what would prevent them from using a teen place, they responded, "little kids, babies." Renée Vaillancourt in *Bare Bones Young Adult Services* advises that a teen room should "not be located next to the children's department. Many young adolescents are just beginning to establish their own identity and resent being perceived as children" (Vaillancourt 2000, 31). Teens have expressed this concern repeatedly in interviews over the years and must be respected in their desire not to be associated with younger children.

If teens reject juxtaposition to children's areas, what do they recommend as desirable neighbors? Proximity of materials and resources was cited by Phoenix teens who wanted a convenient location with a wide variety of resources and popular materials and who preferred using adult collections over children's. Music collections are of special interest to teens, and the King County Library System's newly designed Teen Zone took advantage of the proximity of the adult CD collection to create an edge.

While proximity to desired materials is an important consideration, it should not be confused with a designed edge. Edges clearly signify the boundaries of a place and must contain both the sounds and activities of teens. Advances in sound engineering and acoustic materials allow teens to have music and conversation within their places, and lighting can define areas. It is worth the sacrifice to create a real edge to a teen area and not settle for an imaginary line conveyed by a bookshelf or rug.

Teen places often have distinct edges within their own area. Teens report the need for dual-use rooms. They want a place to be able to work on homework assignments alone or with a group. They also want social areas where they can hang out and relax. While teens never report the need for a quiet space, they do require multiple sound environments for listening to music, viewing a video, and having a group conversation. Again, these interior borders can be accommodated using sound engineering and creative design. Interior borders must be skillfully done and not appear to break up the self-contained whole of the room. This is extremely important in smaller teen spaces.

The last consideration in planning physical place incorporates an overview of the library landscape as a whole. Teen places are not exempt from Clark's requirement that new settlements must "form an allegiance with the land so strong that our existence is seen as an act of adoration, not an act of ruin" (Jensen 2000, 10). We want our teen places to be permanent in our library landscape by being well-integrated into the design of existing or new libraries. This integration of design respects both the library and the teen customer. The notion that posters and furnishings can create place is false. Any authentic teen place demands a total design commitment.

Cultural Place

In a recent interview with Richard Jensen, Elaine asked him to define "culture" as used by W. G. Clark, as well as his own understanding of the term as it relates to place. Jensen said that culture is composed of the things that define us, the physical manifestations of what we as a collective people bring to a place. This "baggage" is born of habit and yet is constantly changing as we adapt to new information and resources. Our cultural objects reveal what we value. We construct our places bringing what we know, what we value, and our tools to continue to refine and rebuild our ever-evolving culture.

Jensen continued the conversation, noting that there are two cultures in planning any library place for teens. The first is the library culture, and the second is the teen culture. Jensen believes there is something comforting about the solid and traditional nature of library culture for teens, and yet, ironically, teen rooms must challenge traditions to be authentic. He concluded that the best teen rooms must convey that the library has made a recognizable sacrifice to provide a place for teens (Meyers, Jensen Interview, 2002).

We agree with Jensen that our look at culture must include both library and teen cultures. In contemplating the approach we would take toward each culture as it related to place, we reflected on library culture as perceived by those who evaluated the PLPYD initiative. In *Public Libraries and Youth Development: A Guide to Practice and Policy,* Samuel Whalen and Joan Costello remark, "Adolescent gregariousness fits poorly with the library's culture of quiet and the policies that protect it. Low-income youth particularly complain of being greeted with suspicion in libraries" (Whalen and Costello 2002, 3). Nicole Yohalem and Karen Pittman echo this theme in their monograph on lessons learned during the PLPYD initiative by identifying a key challenge to libraries as "balancing innovation and tradition" (Yohalem and Pittman 2003, 5). While these cautions and concerns are accurate, we decided that our counter-story should focus on aspects of library culture that foretell a new approach to teen space and a new alignment of values shared by both librarians and teens. We have chosen to tell an optimistic tale of two cultures that meet in public space with more to learn and share than they have had since the last golden age of teen services.

LIBRARY CULTURE

If one were to ask librarians what we know about the culture of the American public library, we would most certainly say that ours is a culture of books, information, and service. If asked to elaborate, we would state that our strengths are in our reference work, our book knowledge, and our willingness to move with the innovations, resources, and efficiencies of technology. If asked what we value, we would say our service. If asked how our community sees us, we would say we are seen as a mainstay of the community's educational, recreational, and cultural activities. If asked about the future of our library culture, we would say that technology is changing our lives so rapidly that the future of the American public library is in many ways up for grabs. This uncertainty about the future is a hallmark of current library culture.

We bring technology and our uncertainty about the future to the way we approach new buildings as well. In a recent report to the Minneapolis Public Library, Bill Sannwald of the San Diego Public Library was asked to comment on building trends and considerations. Sannwald pointed out trends in wireless technology, "intelligent buildings," and "green architecture." He stated that people expect technology as part of the library and that new libraries are growing in size primarily due to technology. Sannwald noted that libraries must be open and flexible spaces ("New Central Library I.C." 2001). Immovable stacks of books forming great warehouses of materials are not images of the future library's culture.

In searching for our future, libraries return to commercial and community models for hints. The Australian librarian Sue Sutherland comments that to draw and secure customers, libraries are adopting techniques used by museums, theme parks, and retail outlets. In their competition for foot traffic, libraries are seeing themselves as destination points and as such are creating and restoring public areas. Cafes, meeting rooms, auditoriums, technology centers, study spaces, and lounge areas abound in new and renovated libraries (Sutherland 2001). The West Bloomfield (Mich.) Public Library has defined its children's area as a destination for families. Indeed, a recent study conducted for the PLA/ALSC's Preschool Literacy Initiative found that many mothers of preschool children visit the library several times a week (Walter 2002). The culture of the library is being redirected to the community, and the library's value as a public meeting place is being renewed.

Both Sannwald and Sutherland recognize the importance of attracting youth and young adults to libraries. Sannwald advises that youth will be attracted to libraries if we create rooms for them, and Sutherland notes an international trend in building libraries specifically for younger customers. "In Singapore, Library@orchard is a lifestyle library for 18 to 35 year olds. Housed in one of the classiest of high rise shopping malls, it has a modern retail look with polished floors, glass, and steel. Music plays, coffee is drunk, and young people find leisure reading from appropriate paperback stacks" (Sutherland 2001). Designing places for teens and early twenty-somethings is emerging as a new element in our library culture.

BUILDING TRENDS FOR TEENS

While the interest in building teen places is fairly new in our library culture, the movement is undeniable. In a recent interview with Cathy Dunn MacRae, Elaine asked what inspired the creation of *Voice of Youth Advocates'* column "YA Spaces of Your Dreams." MacRae recounted being at the 1999 ALA Conference in New Orleans at a multidivision-sponsored program, "Way Cool: Designing Young Adult Spaces that Work." The program was described thus:

> Would you put a couch in your young adult section? Teens see them-selves as "way cool." Do your young adult spaces live up to their expec-tations? Design an area for them that works. This presentation will dis-cuss programming and planning for the young spaces, how to design space for teens in libraries that can be welcoming, inviting, and durable as well as promoting the concept that teen environments can function successfully. (American Library Association 1999)

Waiting for the program to begin, MacRae was dumbfounded as people poured into the hall that held 5,000. Most interesting to MacRae was the pre-ponderance of library administrators who attended and their obvious eager-ness for information on teen spaces. Based on this climate of interest and need, *Voice of Youth Advocates* published the first "YA Spaces of Your Dreams" article in October of that year.

When asked to explain this overwhelming interest in teen spaces, MacRae speculated that demographics or the teen population bulge was one possibility. She also ventured that the surge of teens using library technology was causing libraries to address a need for appropriate space. Teens will not be dissuaded from using the Internet, and an appropriate place must be found for these enthusiastic new clients.

Library professionals are not the only ones aware of the need for new public spaces for teens. In preparation for a fall 2003 capital bond project, the King County Library System conducted public hearings in thirty-eight locations around the county. Hearings were conducted by a team composed of the local library manager, a library administrative liaison, and a community member. As part of the hearings, attendees were asked to rank the most valued library services in a listing. To the amazement of all library staff, the single most valued space in all thirty-eight hearings was a "Teen Zone."

An emerging building boom for teen places in libraries, destination spaces competing for foot traffic in the community, a focus on customer satisfaction and technology, and age-defined user groups all bode well for the institutionalization of teen places. How teens will shape these places leads us to our next cultural investigation.

TEEN CULTURE

Teen culture is enjoying an unparalleled scrutiny in our country. Sadly, much of this attention is fueled not by an interest in developing teens, but in selling to them. In a recent article, Ginger Thomson, chief executive officer and co-founder of DoughNET Inc., a San Francisco-based financial portal for teenagers, reports that "the 31 million teens in the country have a total of $151 billion in annual discretionary income, or $5,000 each on average" (Hackett 2000). The constant marketing of goods to teens has created a variety of cultural values that are both good and bad.

On the upside, teens enjoy the attention and appreciate being courted and catered to as valuable customers. The intense media exposure of teen fashion, music, and competence in technology often affirms their contribution to the larger culture. Elaine's favorite commercials feature teens as technology gurus. On a recent plane trip, the airline video magazine featured a story of two teens who created their own companies—Baby Soft and Red Webs. Teens of all generations have contributed to our musical innovations, and the contributions of rock, rap, hip hop, and heavy metal to our musical heritage are firmly established. Increasingly, the media are providing a positive cultural image of teens and their many talents and contributions.

On the downside, the idea that one's personal worth depends on having the right shoes, clothing, sports or entertainment equipment, make-up, and, by extension, body type has resulted in teens willing to go to destructive extremes to achieve marketed images of beauty and coolness. The desire to sell to teens has created a manipulative environment where the good of the teen is often compromised for the sale. Marketing often masks authentic teen culture, and librarians need to go directly to teens as well as the marketplace if they want to uncover authentic cultural information. We must not fall into the trap of believing our young people are only material girls and guys.

THE ART OF ASKING THE RIGHT QUESTIONS

When the Phoenix Public Library opened Teen Central in April 2001, the public poured into the doors to see this much-touted public place. Teens looked around, liked what they saw, and settled in to view movies, surf the Internet, listen to music, read magazines and books, and just hang out with friends and staff. When adults came in, knowing they couldn't stay because clearly posted signs announced this was for folks twelve to eighteen years old, they wistfully uttered, "I wish they had a place like this when I was a teen. I would have loved it." In short, Teen Central is a culturally authentic teen place that is recognized by those currently in their teen years and those who only recall these years.

When Phoenix library staff and their architectural team of Will Bruder Architects, Ltd., are asked the secret of their success, they talk about a five-step process used to unearth the current culture of Phoenix teens. This process describes five focus groups that the architects and staff conducted in order to determine the final floor plan, lighting, acoustics, furnishings, equipment, service areas, and materials in Teen Central. (See figure 5-2.)

This process is not new to architects; indeed, it lies at the heart of their business and their art. The architect's ability to draw information from teens, or any client, is what allows him to capture the culture of a proposed place. The art of asking the right questions and clarifying ideas by posing follow-up questions defines the best architects. In the case of Teen Central, principal architect Will Bruder is credited with extraordinary talent in this area. Just as the questions and follow-up questions are essential to the process, so is the atmosphere of trust between adults and teens. All answers must be recorded and respected. Group leaders are reminded to begin with a clear statement that this is a brainstorming process and there is no such thing as a "wrong" answer.

What are the right questions? Examples provided during Elaine's interview with Richard Jensen and from focus group notes include the following ones.

1. What do you expect this place to be?
2. Think of your favorite place to be with friends, and name four things that make it a good place to be.

FIGURE 5-2 Phoenix Public Library's Teen Central; "Space for Teens by Teens." Five focus group process used to create Teen Central.

Session One: Service Plan Brainstorming

Architect and teens meet. Architect affirms his commitment to teen customer satisfaction and involvement in the process. (Note: This must be sincere, and if possible select your architect based on his experience and willingness to work with the teen customer. Teen Central would not have been possible without Will Bruder's belief in this process.) Brainstorming session covers room use, features, and activities to be accommodated within the space. Architect and staff take notes to prepare for session two.

Session Two: Refine Service Plan, Design, and Furnishings

Teens vote on features of the room (dance floor, café, CD listening station, living room area, video viewing, individual and group study rooms, art display, PC spaces). Teens vote on furniture (real samples and photos), fabrics, colors, and lighting fixtures.

Session Three: Materials Selection

Teens work with staff and materials vendors to develop collections. A disc jockey leads the music selection discussion while playing various genres of music. A comic store manager provides numerous samples of comic books and graphic novels for teens to review. After a lively discussion, teens vote on types of comics they want in Teen Central collection. This session also includes voting on all other materials for this collection—fiction genres, categories of nonfiction. In addition to discussions, teens complete written surveys on books, authors, movies, CDs, musical groups, and software. This information was the basis of materials selection for this room.

Session Four: Floor Plan

Teens are divided into work groups and provided with scaled-down drawings of furniture and floor plans of a similar scale for the footprint of the room. The architect discusses basic concepts of design and defines the work of the session. Using furniture cutouts and lots of tape, teens work to create their ideal floor plan. Staff and architects are available for consultation, but teens resolve design issues and solve problems independently. Work groups present and defend their designs to the group.

Session Five: Review of Final Floor Plan and Room Naming

Using input from all focus groups, architects create a final floor plan to present and defend before teens. They translate this plan into cardboard bookshelves and computer stations, indicate walls and walkways with masking tape lines on the floor, and use paper cutouts to represent the dance floor and furniture placements. The architect literally walks teens through their improvised space. Teens critique plans and make final suggestions. Teens brainstorm names for the room that were compiled by staff. Teens voted by mail for the name of the room. In spite of the architect's strong preference for another name, the teens were given the final say, and "Teen Central" went up in neon lights.

3. Where do you like to hang out? What do you like about the mall?
4. What interesting things do you want going on in Teen Central?
5. What if we could have a performance space? What kind of performers?
6. What do you like? Music . . . color . . . games?
7. Do you want to be alone or with other people?
8. What do you like to do on computers?
9. What makes a cool place to study?
10. Name something you wish would be in the new teen room.
11. What do you like in furniture—be on the floor? Sprawl? Comfortable? We have some furniture here—test it and tell us what you think.
12. What kind of food should we have in our teen space?

This interactive process should be fun for teens whose opinions are not frequently sought. Phoenix combined questions with testing real furniture, having a disc jockey spin tunes to facilitate the group's selection of CDs, having examples of graphic novels and comics to refine the best choices, and holding discussions of popular literature. After each question-and-answer session, architectural and library staff compiled the teens' responses and created lists of possible options for various categories, from color and music to types of chairs and magazines. Each teen was given five dots and the advice: "Talk is cheap: time to vote and refine your options." Teens were careful with their votes, and a consensus emerged from the voting.

A picture of Phoenix teen culture emerged as teens defined their preferences in music, performance, computer uses, furnishings, performance space, materials, colors, lighting, and social gathering spaces. It is no surprise that many of the videos, CDs, and computer games that were recorded in 2000 are no longer popular. Teen popular culture is ephemeral; and the specific names and responses will change as teens define their tastes differently over time. The social nature of teens is more culturally constant, and the need for teen places to have flexibility to regroup furnishings, clear shelving, create performance space, and accommodate new technologies will not change as quickly as yesterday's singing idol.

The ephemeral nature of teen culture suggests that it would be wise to continuously check with teens on the staying power or current coolness of library teen places. Materials will always be updated as teens remain key participants in selecting library books, video and audio products, magazines, and links to the Internet via library teen websites. However, the choices of colors, furnishings, and program and display areas need to be kept fresh. The good news is that the high use rates of these popular areas mean wear and tear on furnishings. We anticipate that furnishings should need replacement because of their worn condition at about the rate that they lose their "cool-ness." The inherent flexibility designed into teen spaces should allow for the reorganization of materials and furniture to accommodate new program and service needs.

Spiritual or Evocative Place

Successful teen places must attain the third dimension of successful place—the spiritual or evocative. W. G. Clark writes, "We look to the spiritual or evocative for images that strengthen the architecture, making it memorable in the landscape" (Jensen 2000, 14). A visit to the Los Angeles County Public Library's Teen'Scape web page reveals much about the evocative nature of place: "The name 'Teen'Scape' is meant to convey both sanctuary for and ownership by teenagers." Los Angeles teens are sheltered by the tentlike fabric arches above them as they enter Teen'Scape and are free to roam areas devoted to materials, computers, and comfortable social spaces for listening, viewing, talking, or working together. The service desk is tucked behind the living room area and has the feel of the table that a DJ would set up at a mixer. Library staff are accessible, but the feeling is that teens hold the reins. We encourage readers to visit the Los Angeles Public Library's website (http:// www.lapl.org/teenscape/library/teenscape.html) to view photos of this inno-vative place.

While the spiritual aspect of place is the most elusive, it is also the aspect that is most memorable and has the power to draw teens back again and again. The evocative nature of Phoenix's Teen Central is fostered by the free-flowing curves of walls and walkways, the juxtaposition of soft fiberglass col-ors with stainless steel, and the excitement of neon and halogen lights. There is just the right mix of what some might deem incongruent materials to prove that rules can be challenged to create new and wondrous worlds. As a cornu-copia of different chairs and furnishings are rearranged daily by the teens, the place affirms the need to bring a variety of styles together and to continue to invent new constructs within a space that honors experimentation. Two glass vistas in Teen Central bind the room to the city of Phoenix. One is a cityscape looking north with a view up Central Avenue, and the second reveals the interior of the library leading to the "crystal canyon" at the building's core. These vistas evoke the heart of the library and the connection to a city that spans a range of commerce, culture, and development that will be shaped by the teens at work and play in this place. We again encourage you to visit the

Phoenix Public Library website (http://www.phoenixteencentral.org/teen central/frame.html) to view photos of Teen Central.

When trying to fathom the genesis of this evocative place, it occurred to Elaine that success in this area belongs to the architect alone. While the evocative image was originally suggested by teen customers, the ability to understand the magic of line, light, vistas, materials, and the juxtaposition of functions and forms in realizing these images is the architect's domain. When one listens to Will Bruder talk, one is struck by his use of imagery. In an interview before the opening of Phoenix's Central Library, Bruder remarked, "Architecture has its pragmatic side, but it also needs to be a search for poetic possibilities . . . For me, it's from the heart to the mind to the hand. I'm always striving to create sensuous experiences that get to the imagination of everyone" (Nilsen 1995).

The best advice for finding an architect with this ability is to listen carefully to his or her descriptions of existing buildings and stories of working with clients. To create evocative places for teens, the architect must be able to draw information from the teen clients. This architect must also be able to understand the culture of the existing library and community. Most importantly, the architect must be able to remember the radical changes and responsibilities faced by those in the second decade of life and provide images of possibility, shelter, and the ability to matter in this space and in the larger world.

While a mighty challenge, an evocatively successful space will be rewarded by teens who attach themselves to it and remember time spent and thoughts and dreams nurtured in it. In a recent interview with Shera Farnham, the head of the Phoenix Public Library's branch libraries, Elaine was fascinated by Farnham's description of working with architects on library and personal design projects. She discussed the process of drawing information from the client and then waiting for the architect's final plan. Farnham referred to the need to make a "leap of faith" when the architectural plans call for new materials, designs, and layouts that seem unorthodox and yet somehow very right. Success in creating spiritual or evocative place does rely on courage or "faith" in what Will Bruder refers to as the "heart" of the architect. It also depends on library staff willing to provide the highest level of design for the teen customer.

IMPLICATIONS

Richard Jensen's statement that teens recognize when the library has made "significant sacrifice" to provide exciting teen place bears repeating. The heart of such sacrifice captures the implications of place in building a lasting future for teen service in the public library. The first part of our sacrifice is a square footage allocation for permanent teen space. The second sacrifice is sharing power with teens as they serve as key cultural informants revealing what is important and lasting in their culture. When teens reveal that music, video, comfortable furnishings, and food are key cultural elements, we must be willing to not only hear their message, but be willing to act on it in our teen places. Lastly, we must be willing to take risks architecturally. If a design authentically reflects teen culture, it will be radical in some way. We must be willing to take a "leap of faith" to assure that our places will be memorable and evoke the best in action and thought from our teens.

Courage in the provision and design of teen places has implications for all our library work. A common response among customers of any age when confronted with successful teen places is "Why can't we have something like this?" The desire to be listened to, to have food available, to have music, to take part in the selection of materials, the desire for exciting and responsive public spaces—these desires are all age-neutral. The process of asking the right questions is at the heart of all library place planning, and the challenge of one well-executed space is to create others of equal value. The value of public space unifies teen and library culture and helps libraries prepare for future services and facilities.

The best library teen places have started with genuine conversations between young adults, librarians, architects, and designers. Those teen voices are new to the public library narrative, and they form a counter-story of its own which we will explore in the next chapter.

CHAPTER 6

Conversation

The Power of Teen Voices

The counter-story told in this chapter began when the Wallace–Reader's Digest Fund provided a year for Public Libraries as Partners in Youth Development libraries to talk to teens in their communities, talk to community partners, and talk among themselves. One of the most amazing aspects of this story is the uniformity of teen voices within the tale. Whether the teens lived in large urban centers, isolated rural towns, spoke English or another language, were poor or had adequate resources, and used the library frequently or hardly ever, they spoke with one voice about their experiences with public libraries and their dreams for improved services. They asked libraries to provide cooler places, more technology, friendlier staff, better hours, and more student-friendly policies. They offered to help us create a new future and indeed predicted that the only way this story would have a happy ending is if they were active participants in our drama.

We have mentioned that Elaine captured this story in the article "The Coolness Factor." What we have not told is the lesson she learned in creating the article's title. Her original suggestion was "The Coolness Factor: Ten Libraries Talk to Teens." When Joey Rodger, Urban Library Council president and Elaine's supervisor, read the draft of the article, she wisely commented. "Don't you really mean ten libraries *listen* to teens? What is the point of talking if you don't listen? We talk to teens all the time; this time we listened and as a result *did* something." The power of listening is found in the inherent promise to respond. The power of teen voices springs from youthful passion and commands attention by its straightforward and authentic style. When teens speak in one voice, we must pay special attention.

In this chapter, we will look at conversation in three ways. First, we will examine the nature of conversation using the work of Theodore Zeldin as a base for our discussion. Second, we will discuss the power of teen voices and our professional responsibility to provide opportunities for teens to find and use their voice. Last, we will look at a new technique for having conversations called "The World Café" and the results of applying this technique to create a Library Teen Bill of Rights.

THEODORE ZELDIN

In his book *Conversation: How Talk Can Change Our Lives,* Theodore Zeldin proposes that the "twenty-first century needs a new ambition, to develop not talk but conversation, which does change people. Real conversation catches fire. It involves more than sending and receiving information" (Zeldin 1998, 1–3). Zeldin sees conversation as the pivot of change for our age. He bases his theory on historical evidence of people changing "the subject of their conversation, or the way they talked, or the persons they talked to." He gives examples of history changing when women began to talk first to each other and then to society at large about their needs. The revolution of feminism continues to change history. Conversations about race resulted in the civil rights movement and ongoing societal change.

The potential of a new conversation is always change. We share Zeldin's excitement about a process that "is a meeting of minds with different memories and habits. When minds meet, they don't just exchange facts: they transform them, reshape them, draw different implications from them, engage in new trains of thought. Conversation doesn't just reshuffle the cards: it creates new cards" (Zeldin 1998, 14).

Listening

Zeldin believes that conversations depend on listening and offers wonderful insight into the process of teens and adults needing new rules for listening. He provides a marvelous quote from a seventeen-year-old boy talking about conversation at home:

> I feel patronized in every conversation with my parents. They think they are superior. They treat me at a low intellectual level. I have much better conversations with my friends. So I don't really put in the effort for a real conversation at home. Dad never really listens. Mom has to take center stage without being interrupted. I think it's legitimate to interrupt: it shows interest. It's better with my friends because they treat me as a peer, and they get impassioned about things, which parents don't. A

conversation should be fueled by the passion that we have for the subject. (Zeldin 1998, 33)

Like many young adults, Zeldin's seventeen-year-old is succinct in identifying the issues in effective listening. A careful listener can extract some great truths from the above quote. We would like to paraphrase what the teen is saying and construct some basic rules of good listening.

Do not adopt a superior attitude. Respect is the foundation of conversation.

Do assume that the teen has the intellectual capacity for the conversation.

Make sure you are listening. Teens always know if you are faking.

Leave your ego at home. This is not time for you to be "center stage" but to draw the teens out.

Don't assume interruption is a sign of disrespect; it more likely is enthusiasm. If you want to establish guidelines for formal conversation, make sure that everyone understands and abides by them. Work with teens to establish these guidelines.

Choose a subject that you and the teen can feel passionate about. Ask important and interesting questions. Create a context for the importance of the information. The fact that the library needs to know something does not intrinsically make the subject interesting to a teen. Prepare background information and convey context to create interest in the topic and perhaps passion in the conversation.

In following a discussion on a teen advisory council's electronic discussion list (TAGAD-L-TAG Advisor Discussion), Elaine watched with interest and concern as a librarian who was working with a teen advisory group continued to pose questions to the other adults about how to improve teen participation in her group. She followed all the adult suggestions and finally signed off in despair, thanking the group for ideas but giving up on the teens that refused to participate. We suspect the problem was not her willingness to have a conversation about the issues; it was her choice of people for the conversation. She should have been talking to teens and carefully listening to their opinions. We would guess that the teens had become bored with the topics of interest to their advisor. If given time for discussion and opportunities for genuine input, they might have come up with projects that would have captured their attention and sparked their participation.

Just as the architects in chapter 5 constructed the right set of questions to begin a conversation about the nature of teen place, we need to construct the right questions for conversations about teen services and programs. A favorite example of how *not* to create these questions occurred during a conversation on evaluation in the first year of the PLPYD initiative. Elaine transformed the example, provided by George D'Elia, into a story about a mythical cafeteria worker who was charged with creating a high school lunch menu. In trying to decide what to serve, the cafeteria worker decided to ask her customers what they wanted. Her first set of questions included simple ones like "Would you rather have broccoli, squash, or cauliflower for lunch?" When she tabulated the results, she discovered that 45 percent of the students said they would rather have broccoli. However, when she served broccoli the next day, only a few students ate it. She then realized the real question should be "What vegetables would you like us to serve at lunch?" This question led to the creation of a highly successful salad bar in the student cafeteria.

While humorous, the flaw of ineffective question construction is at the heart of why so many questions do not lead to conversations that enable us to connect and make needed changes. Effective questions can be as basic as "What should we stop doing?" "What should we keep doing?" or "What should we start doing?" Teens in Tucson, Arizona, met with their congressman, Ed Pastor. In preparation for their conversation, Pastor provided teens with three questions:

1. What do you think are the three most important social problems that affect teenagers today?
2. How do you think these social problems could or should be resolved?
3. Who could or should be responsible for solving these problems?

Good conversations can only be predicated on good questions.

THE POWER OF TEEN VOICES

The power of teen voices was heard throughout the Public Libraries as Partners in Youth Development initiative. Teen voices provided the interest, content, and color of Elaine's two "Coolness" articles published in *American Libraries* in 1999 and 2001. When it became evident to Elaine that teen voices were the most powerful voices for telling the PLPYD story, she began to test her theory on the initiative's library participants. They reported that they were using teens more and more to tell their local stories, and teens were increasingly quoted by local and national reporters. PLPYD staff agreed that teen voices were the most powerful in telling the story of the impact of library work. Chapin Hall and the Forum for Youth Investment rely on teen voices in their evaluations of the PLPYD project. Most simply, these are the voices that matter.

One quality of teen conversation that often distinguishes it from adult discourse is the ability of teens to get to the point of a story quickly. Teens are masterful in their ability to "make a long story short." In getting to the point, they frequently reveal the most important message in a story. It was not unusual for Elaine to be listening to teens and realize that they understood a key aspect of a program that she had not yet grasped.

An excellent example of this occurred during the PLPYD's first program at the ALA Annual Conference in Chicago in the summer of 2001. The program was titled "Cool Jobs for Kids at the Library" and featured six teens from three PLPYD libraries. During a panel discussion, these teens not only described their jobs as we had requested them, but quickly got to the real point of the cool jobs story. With moving conviction, teens ended their description of their library work by saying that the most important part of their job was not the salary but the positive impact of their work on the community. Teens explained to the professional audience:

> I see more positive things when I'm with the community. And I feel like I have an impact every day. The library makes you more knowledgeable, while you're helping kids. And you can honor the other people there who are trying to help.   —Nineteen-year-old boy

> I get to be a role model. If they need help with computers or just want to talk, I know I can make their day better. There was a boy I helped, Isaiah, a kid who liked to play around and not do his homework. One day I helped him with his project. A few days later he returned to say he got an "A" on his project. Now every time he has a project, he comes into the library and says, "Well, we got another one!"
> —Sixteen-year-old girl

> When I was a little kid, nobody helped me at the library. I want to revolutionize services for kids.   —Sixteen-year-old girl

> I show people that it doesn't matter what neighborhood you come from . . . there's something for you at the library . . . At least once in your life, you should have a job that helps you give back to your community.
> —Twelve-year-old girl

> (Urban Libraries Council 2001)

The impact of these teen voices was to affirm the work for library participants, solidify the understanding and commitment of the many library directors and administrators in the audience, and convince non-initiative sites to work with teens in new ways.

Teens have participated in every PLPYD training or informational program since that first success in Chicago. Program evaluations always mention the portion of the program delivered by teens as one of the most helpful and meaningful. The effort of working with teachers to get school release time, developing procedures for teens to travel to conferences, and taking the time to develop speaking and presentation skills so that teens will be prepared and professional for their audiences was always rewarded during the PLPYD years. The "Toolkit" that comprises part 4 of this book provides a protocol for conducting a teen forum; this protocol gives some guidance for libraries wanting to listen to their teens in a formal setting.

Phoenix Voices

In 1998 the city of Phoenix instituted a Youth Budget Hearing as part of the annual citizens' budget review. The purpose of the Youth Budget Hearing is for youth to learn about the budget and talk directly to city staff and council members about what city services are most important to them. From 1998 to the present, teens from the Library Teen Council and teen library users have been present at these meetings to tell their stories and thank the council for services that have particular relevance in their lives. When Elaine returned to public service work, she continued to test the theories of youth development in the real world of Phoenix's Teen Central. While very familiar with past youth participation in budget hearings, she was anxious to have teens tell stories about the newest of Phoenix's youth services.

In discussions with Teen Central staff, Elaine asked them to recommend teens who could best give voice to the room. The staff recommended two teens who were not typical library users before the opening of Teen Central. Both teens had been transformed by their contact with library staff and services in the first year of Teen Central. The following is a transcript provided by Mathew Fowler of his budget hearing testimony.

> Hi. My name is Mathew Fowler, people have always called me the Sandman. I came to Teen Central about one and a half years ago. Before that I never knew of such a thing. I was always under the influence of mind altering substances. That was until the staff started to get involved

in my life, I started to see life sober. The people up here at Teen Central touch me and gave me a hand to help my self up. Even though I am 19 now, I stop by to say thanks.

I believe every library should have a teen center. It takes kids that are in my place and shows them that there is something better out there. It is a safe hang out spot that is drug free. Give a place that is fun and it is easy to study for school. The people here are nice and are very helpful. If every library had a teen center, the kids will be kids once again. (Fowler 2002)

"[T]he kids will be kids once again." When Elaine read these lines from Matt's transcript, she was transfixed and changed in the way that authentic voices always change us. Matt's words enabled her to see things differently and to gain new understanding. Elaine realized that Matt understood that the circumstances of his youth were not the way things should be. She also realized that she has never seen Matt angry, and indeed, she marveled at his positive approach to the people and resources at the library. When asked to speak at the budget hearing, Matt did not consider the inconvenience of the request to his own work schedule, or regard it as one more pressure added to a life dominated by the struggle to find a place to live and resist the daily temptations to return to drugs offered by those living on the streets. Instead, he asked if his remarks should be written down and for hints on how to do a good job with this assignment. We are inspired whenever we reread Matt's statement, and so were those in attendance at the city budget hearing. There is no one on the professional staff at the Phoenix Public Library who could have been more effective than Matt in stating the impact of Teen Central.

LIBRARY TEEN BILL OF RIGHTS

The notion of asking teens to create a Library Teen Bill of Rights emerged when we first discussed teen participation in this book. The voice of teens is featured throughout our *Rumble Fish* section, but we wanted a document that was the sole creation of teens and would give shape to our final metanarrative. The task for creating this document fell to the Youth Partnership Council of the Public Libraries as Partners in Youth Development initiative. A committee of senior teen leaders from the Youth Partnership Council worked not only to create a final bill of rights, but to create the process needed for teens to do this work. A short review of the process will capture our conversation leading to the final bill.

Initial Conversation

Our conversation with senior teen leaders began with the question, "What is a bill of rights?" This is obviously a question that most of us could not begin to discuss without some background and enforces a key principle of conversation with teens. It is the responsibility of the adult to prepare the needed background information for conversations that teens do not initiate. It is also prudent to listen during the sharing of this background information in order to gauge teens' interest in the subject. If they are truly not interested, you cannot expect much of an exchange.

We were fascinated with our advisory group's critique of background articles we had provided on bills of rights. We followed their advice in how we would prepare the larger group of teens. The quality of guidance from the teens is captured in a critique of background sites by one of our teen leaders, as provided in figure 6-1. Our conversation with our teens took place during phone conferences and via e-mail. During our phone conference, the teen leadership struggled with how to define and explain to other teens what we wanted in a Library Teen Bill of Rights. All agreed that the features of a bill of rights should include:

- what every teen is entitled to in a library—what naturally they should expect as a user
- what no library should refuse to provide
- what rights apply to individual teens and teens as a group
- guidelines for when individual rights are superseded by the good of the group—i.e., someone can't shout "fire" in a crowded theater.

The group also concurred that for a right to be included it must be perceived as a universal right. They defined this universality as a right that was easily agreed upon by the group and was not the subject of heated debate.

Questions from our initial discussion of this bill of rights continued to emerge and spark further conversations. What is the difference between a "right" and a "want"? How can we be sure that we who have worked in libraries for the past four years and have become advocates have the perspective needed to speak for all teens? How can we ensure that adults do not dominate the process? And finally, how can we create language that speaks to teens—yet is understandable and authentic for our peers? These questions framed our conversations and led us deeper into an understanding of the magnitude of our task.

FIGURE 6-1   Teens' critique of background sources for the
Library Teen Bill of Rights

1. Wisconsin Department of Public Instruction's Bill of Rights for All Students
   www. dpi.state.wi.us/dpi/dlsea/equity/eqbor.html

   It's not in complete sentences!! (Sorry, first thing I noticed.) I think this one is good for giving a general idea of what the Bill of Rights is supposed to be, but it is a bit long, and the language seems quite formal. If I had to choose three from this list, this would be the third one.

2. Brookline Youth Lacrosse Player Bill of Rights
   http://home.attbi. com/~scottrunnr/playerRights.htm

   I think this one is really good. The sentences are short and to the point, and the choice of words makes it easy for youth to understand. I also like how the ideas they present look at all aspects of the lacrosse players—they address both the players' and coaches' responsibilities and their relationships with one another. I think this should be one of the examples that gets sent out.

3. Youth Bill of Rights from National Child Rights Alliance
   www.parent.net/facts/archive/youthrights.shtml

   I like the layout of this one too, because it has the general idea as a heading, and then it goes into the descriptions below. I don't think we'd have enough time to do something like that though, so it may be pointless to show them this. They might think we'd have to do something as long and thought out as this one, when we're just doing a short list of rights (or at least that's my impression of our activity). So, for our purposes, maybe not.

4. ALA's Library Bill of Rights
   www.ala.org

   I like this because it's short, but the language is kind of formal and adulty-like (for lack of better words at the moment). I think that maybe we could send this just to show delegates what the library has, and then one or two of the youth examples to show more of what we're looking for. (Side note—it might be interesting, just to show the applications of these Bill of Rights documents, to send this one with one of the interpretations that they provide here: http://www.ala.org/work/freedom/interprt.html. I read the one on "Free Access to Libraries for Minors"— quite interesting, though I think I have a weird concept of interesting, so I don't know if the others would like it. The interpretations might seem quite long.)

(Continued)

FIGURE 6-1 (Cont'd)

---

5. ACLU's Briefing Paper Number 9: The Bill of Rights: A Brief History
www.aclu.org/library/pbp9.html

I'm sorry, but I couldn't even get to the end. Not because of the length (though it is quite long), but because it brought back bad memories of 11th grade U.S. History Honors. *shudder* I don't know if knowing all of this history of the U.S. Bill of Rights is really necessary for what we're doing. I don't know how many people would actually want to read this. (No, I'm really not trying to get out of re-"learning" my U.S. History. . . . it's just . . . ugh. I'd rather not.)

I don't know if that helps any or if that's what you were looking for when you said "write us about what you think about them," but if it's not, I am quite reachable by e-mail during the day. (The cubicle they gave me is on the other side of the floor, which is completely empty. It's far away from all my supervisors . . . *grin*) So if my rambling doesn't make sense or you need anything else, let me know.

Oh, and I just remembered the wording of that sign in Chinatown that I was telling you guys about over the phone—it's "It's a privilege to drive. It's a right to walk."

Ok . . . have a wonderful day! Talk to you soon!

—Nineteen-year-old female student

The issue of language prompted the committee to refer to the American Library Association's Library Bill of Rights. Teens commented that many young people might need dictionaries to help them understand the statement, "Materials should not be proscribed or removed because of partisan or doctrinal disapproval." It was decided that an initial activity would be to break the group up into six small committees and have each committee rewrite in teen-friendly language the existing ALA Library Bill of Rights. The teen leadership team also decided that teens needed to do some homework before our conversation, and a packet of information was sent to all teen delegates who would be attending the meetings.

The World Café Process

Teens had identified key questions for our work and had done a wonderful job of selecting materials for a background package that all delegates would use. They assured us that the subject could be made interesting to teens and agreed to be our cheerleaders and warm up the crowd on the morning we would create our Library Teen Bill of Rights. What was missing was a process for quickly engaging teens in conversation and making sure that all voices were heard during the three hours we had for the project. As luck would have it, this void was filled by a youth development meeting held in Phoenix and Elaine's introduction there to the World Café Community.

The World Café Community provides a process to "create a living network of conversation around questions that matter. A Café Conversation is a creative process for leading collaborative dialogue, sharing knowledge and creating possibilities for action in groups of all sizes" ("World Café" 2003). Elaine first experienced the process as a participant in a group of adults and teens in Phoenix. She was fascinated by how quickly the group got to a very high level of discussion and how the ability to move from one conversation to another clarified her thinking on a topic. The World Café has an excellent reference guide available on its website (http://www.theworldcafe.com//), and we encourage you to download their "Café to Go: A Quick Reference Guide for Putting Conversations to Work."

The principles of the World Café are "to clarify the context, create hospitable spaces, explore questions that matter, encourage everyone's contribution, connect diverse perspectives and listen for insights and share discoveries" ("World Café" 2003). We had already clarified the context with our teen leadership group, and the pre-meeting packet of information provided context for all teen participants. The next task was to "create a hospitable space," which we did by arranging the room as suggested in a café style and blanketing the walls with appropriate quotations and ideas. We provided ample art materials for youth to work with at each table as they listened and considered the opinions of their peers. As teens served as table hosts, rotated from table to table, and followed guidelines for listening "deeply," they considered three basic questions:

1. What is a bill of rights?
2. What can we learn from the ALA's Library Bill of Rights that will help us create a Library Teen Bill of Rights?
3. What will we put in our Library Teen Bill of Rights?

We have provided a full description of this process in part 4 of this book.

The end of this counter-story is a happy one. In less than three hours, the teens produced our Library Teen Bill of Rights. (See figure 6-2.)

FIGURE 6-2 Library Teen Bill of Rights

Teens have the right to choose materials for teens at the library.

Teens have the right to use the library despite origin, background, and views.

Teens have the right to use all library materials for the purposes of interest, information, and enlightenment.

Teens have the right to a space and exhibits just for them, and within this space teens should be allowed to have freedom.

Teens have the right to have access to all technology in the library.

Teens have the right to access information as quickly and efficiently as possible.

Teens have the right to offer an opinion for change in the library.

Teens with disabilities should be able to move just as freely as everyone else throughout the library.

Teens have the right to a safe environment.

Teens should be respected as responsible young adults.

All teens should be open-minded to all types of learning.

Libraries should cooperate with all teens and teens should cooperate with adults and peers.

Teens have the right to respect all library materials.

Teens should be treated equally and fairly and not stereotyped.

Teens have the right to have representation in library administrative roles.

All patrons reserve the right to fight the censorship of any and all books and media.

Created by the Public Libraries as Partners in Youth Development project's Youth Partnership Council, July 28, 2002

We believe this document speaks for itself. Nonetheless, we would like to share some questions that continued to plague teens who worked on the bill of rights.

Teens frequently debated the role of parental consent in their access to all library materials. The complexity of access to all materials for minors was not lost on the group. While the majority easily agreed that access was a right for teens, the discussion was excellent and all teens respected the feelings of those youth who advocated more parental supervision.

The second debate was over the question of whether the provision of teen space is a right or a "want." While this was not a heated debate, we were struck by teens questioning their right to a public space. The teen leadership group had wondered if the group's atypical knowledge of the inner workings of public libraries would somehow hamper their ability to speak for all teens. The PLPYD teens clearly understood that library space was at a premium in many of their libraries and were compassionate about the need to displace an existing service in order to create a new teen place. They also wondered if teens have a right to know about all formats for information, instead of just defaulting to the preferred electronic format or the Internet.

These ongoing questions provide a great starting place for conversations with all teens. We suggest that you begin with this Library Teen Bill of Rights and discuss it with teens in your community. The voices of your teens will give you insight into their knowledge of your library and will guide you in creating service plans and policies that truly meet the needs of your community's teens.

CHAPTER 7

Evaluation

The Power of Accountability

The evaluation story is one that Ginny and Elaine have told many times before. We were both part of the initiative to produce output measures for library services for children and teens during the 1990s (Walter 1992; Walter 1995). However, we suspect that our story has not reached a very wide audience. *Output Measures and More: Planning and Evaluating Public Library Services for Young Adults* (Walter 1995) is out of print and apparently out of mind. Evidently, how-to-do-it manuals did not strike a chord with already overworked young adult librarians or generalists. Therefore, we are going to try to tell a different kind of evaluation story here—not so much how to do it, but how to think about it. And we are going to embed the evaluation theme within the larger saga of advocacy.

Advocacy is a concept that resonates for many professionals who champion young adult services in libraries. It has come to suggest speaking out on behalf of those who presumably cannot speak for themselves. Some typical forms of advocacy have included lobbying influential parties, mounting promotional campaigns, and political action of various kinds. There is always an implicit purpose of "getting the message out." The message about young adult library services has been primarily normative, stating that libraries should serve teens because it is the right thing to do. For the most part, this message has not been data-driven, although there has been some effort to leverage statistics about the high level of young adult library usage and the scarcity of young adult librarians to serve them.

In our evaluation story, we would like to link accountability with advocacy. We believe that by using more systematic and sophisticated evaluation tools, we may be able to demonstrate a level of accountability that will create a new counter-story. This is the story of the savvy librarian getting a high return on the taxpayers' investment by meeting the demands of her customers in a growing and desirable market.

Librarians who are able to produce evaluation data that is credible and convincing about the outputs and outcomes of their work with young adults have an incredible advantage when it comes to telling their story to decision-makers. They can demonstrate that what they do makes a positive difference in the lives of young adults they serve and in the community.

SOME CHALLENGES

We acknowledge that there are some challenges facing the librarian who wants to use more effective evaluation initiatives. These include administrative indifference, lack of resources, and lack of technical skills. A further challenge is the fact that library services guided by the youth development principles and practices that we advocate in this book present particular difficulties in conceptualizing, implementing, and interpreting evaluation strategies.

Administrative Indifference

It may be surprising to some that administrators would be indifferent to librarians' desire to evaluate their services. Aren't administrators the ones who usually require that staff document their work? Not always. Sometimes systematic data collection in a library will yield results that are unpalatable to some parties. Administrators may not want to encourage the kind of internal competition for resources that evaluation activities can sometimes generate. An aggressive youth services librarian armed with the evidence that teens make up the bulk of the reference desk activity during after-school hours can look like a shark following a trail of blood.

However, most administrators do acknowledge the desirability of having data for management decision-making and concede that data about results are required by funders. Young adult librarians should watch for the opportunity to demonstrate their willingness to document their services and programs and their ability to mount a sophisticated evaluation effort. They may be able to take the lead when library directors are looking for staff with this kind of expertise.

Lack of Resources

Lack of resources has killed many well-intentioned evaluation efforts. The well-documented paucity of young adult specialists in public libraries means that there are fewer people available to do the work. Generalists are less likely to be motivated to put the effort into evaluating services for a particular population of library users. As we shall see, outcome measurement requires a more intensive effort than the relatively easy data collection and analysis needed for doing output measurement. Good evaluation requires consistency and follow-through that may be difficult to maintain in a library whose staff is stretched to the limit.

This is a tough problem to address, especially in tough budget times. However, the kind of data that evaluation activities produce is particularly valuable when hard decisions about resource allocation have to be made. We have found that more and more librarians are building evaluation into grant requests, thus making it possible to hire outside consultants to do the work. Hiring outside evaluators also has the advantage of making the results more credible, since there is less likelihood of internal bias distorting the data or the interpretation.

Lack of Technical Skills

We have heard librarians complain that they would make more of an effort to conduct evaluation studies if they were more confident of their research skills. They are intimidated by the need to do scientific sampling, appropriate surveys, and mathematical calculations. They wonder about the acceptability of "softer" qualitative techniques such as focus groups and interviews.

We are sympathetic. We had hoped that *Output Measures and More: Planning and Evaluating Public Library Services for Young Adults* would help to demystify the basic elements of data collection and analysis. We still believe that a motivated librarian can turn to that or other similar manuals, take it a step at a time, and collect the data that measure the basic outputs of her services to teens. However, we acknowledge that the bar has been raised by the more recent call for outcome measures.

OUTCOME MEASURES

Output measures are designed to answer the questions "how many?" or "how much?" Outcome measures, on the other hand, are intended to answer the question, "so what?" You may have circulated 5,000 young adult books last year, five for every teen in your community. That is a basic output measure. If you want to know what difference those 5,000 books meant to the teens that checked them out, you are in the realm of outcome measures. You are trying to determine the outcomes, or the impacts, of your services.

Outcomes are usually defined as the benefits or changes for individuals or populations during or after participating in particular program activities. An excellent discussion of outcome measures can be found in a United Way publication, *Measuring Program Outcomes: A Practical Approach* (1996). The Institute for Museum and Library Services has also produced manuals and training opportunities for librarians who want to learn more about how to do this.

The established methods for answering the "so what" question are more sophisticated than those that can be used to calculate outputs. Many of the outcomes that library services are designed to produce are subjective and difficult to measure by any means. How does one measure the pleasure derived from reading a well-wrought mystery novel? Or the pride experienced by a teen who has helped a senior citizen use the Internet for the first time? Or the impact of that library work experience on that teen's future job opportunities?

Fortunately, it is not quite as difficult as it sounds. In order to measure outcomes, you really only need to know two things:

1. your outcome targets, i.e., your objectives for a program's level of achievement; and
2. your outcome indicators, i.e., data that measure how well a program is achieving an outcome.

You may be trying to measure benefits or changes to teens during the program or service if it is an ongoing activity, or you may be measuring benefits or changes to teens after a particular program is over.

If you measure at some point during the course of a program, you are taking a snapshot of the outcomes at a particular point in time. If you are trying to determine outcomes after a program is over, or after an individual's participation in the program has ended, you also need to have some "before" data. Otherwise, you won't know if any changes have occurred. This usually involves some kind of pre-test/post-test research design and is most useful for measuring a limited program with specific objectives, such as a training program. Figure 7-1 outlines some sample outcomes and outcome indicators for youth participation and youth employment programs in public libraries.

You can probably see some of the difficulties inherent in measuring outcomes. If you are going to measure changes or benefits to individuals, you usually have to get that information directly from them. This means asking questions we have not traditionally asked our library customers. However, we believe that we will actually improve the quality of our relationship with teens who use our services if we become accustomed to dealing with them in

FIGURE 7-1   Sample outcomes and outcome indicators for young adult library programs

---

Youth Participation Programs

Desired outcome: Participants increase their knowledge of library's mission and services.

> *Outcome indicator:* Number and percentage of participants in program who increase their scores on pre-test/post-test (written survey or interview) about library's mission and services.

Desired outcome: Participants increase their leadership and interpersonal skills.

> *Outcome indicator:* Number and percentage of participants in program who increase their scores on pre-test/post-test (written survey or interview) about basic leadership and interpersonal communication principles.

> *Outcome indicator:* Number and percentage of participants in program who report (through written survey or interview) involvement in other community or school service activities after beginning participation in the program.

> *Outcome indicator:* Documentation through observation of specific desired behavior changes in participants by program leaders or directors. This is a qualitative indicator that can be used in conjunction with other quantitative measures.

Youth Employment Programs

Desired outcome: Participants acquire designated job skills.

> *Outcome indicator:* Number and percentage of participants in program who demonstrate competence in the designated job skills—i.e., regular on-time attendance, appropriate communication skills, computer use, public service attitudes.

Desired outcome: Participants acquire knowledge of employment opportunities.

> *Outcome indicator:* Number and percentage of participants who are able to articulate (through written survey or interview) reasonable short-term and future employment opportunities.

> *Outcome indicator:* Number and percentage of participants who are able to correctly name the required training for two or more desired careers.

Desired outcome: Participants acquire positive personal education goals.

> *Outcome indicator:* Number and percentage of participants who report through pre-test/post-test surveys or interviews enhanced and more specific educational goals after beginning (or completion) of program.

---

this one-to-one fashion. It is a more customized approach, more like the best of our reference services and more like the kind of individualized services that other professionals such as doctors, lawyers, and social workers provide.

Evaluating Library Homework Assistance Programs: A Case Study

We believe that it won't be long before librarians and researchers will collaborate on the creation of easy-to-use models for determining outcomes of many basic library services. We also hope that good national studies will be conducted that local libraries can use as reference points.

Virginia Walter and Cindy Mediavilla received the first ALA Research Grant to develop models for evaluating the outcomes of library homework assistance programs. As a conceptual framework, we used the six outcomes of positive youth development that were synthesized and articulated by the Public Libraries as Partners in Youth Development project. We have referred to them elsewhere in this book but include them here again for convenience. These outcomes, which are necessary for teens to make the healthy transition from childhood to adulthood, are as follows:

1. Youth contribute to their community.
2. They feel safe in their environment.
3. They have meaningful relationships with adults and peers.
4. They achieve educational success.
5. They develop marketable skills.
6. They develop personal and social skills.

These two UCLA researchers developed a survey instrument designed to elicit whether any of these outcomes had occurred as a result of participation in a library homework assistance program. They tested the survey instrument as an interview or focus group schedule and as a written questionnaire at a number of libraries throughout the country: Fort Wayne, Ind.; Philadelphia, Pa.; Monterey County, Oakland, and Culver City, Calif.; Tucson, Ariz.; and King County, Wash. The instrument yielded interesting data from interviews and focus groups and as a written survey. It was used with teens, staff, and parents. Optimally, libraries would be able to triangulate the data from the self-reporting of the teen with the observations of the staff and parents. Figure 7-2 is the survey instrument designed to be used with a teen who works in a homework center.

FIGURE 7-2 Homework Center Survey for teen homework helpers

Please circle the answer for each statement that best describes how you feel about it. After you have circled an answer, please write a sentence or two explaining your answer.

1. When I work in the Homework Center, I am doing something good for the community.

   Agree   Disagree   Don't know

   Explain: _____

   _____

   _____

2. I feel safe when I am in the library.

   Agree   Disagree   Don't know

   Explain: _____

   _____

   _____

3. When I am helping in the Homework Center, I have an opportunity to work with adults in a positive way.

   Agree   Disagree   Don't know

   Explain: _____

   _____

   _____

4. When I help in the Homework Center, I have an opportunity to work in a positive way with people my own age.

   Agree   Disagree   Don't know

   Explain: _____

   _____

   _____

5. Working at the Homework Center helps me do well in school.

   Agree   Disagree   Don't know

   Explain: _____

   _____

   _____

6. I learn things while working at the Homework Center that will help me get a good job someday.

Agree   Disagree   Don't know

Explain: _____

_____

_____

7. I learn how to get along with people better while working at the Homework Center.

Agree   Disagree   Don't know

Explain: _____

_____

_____

Ginny and Cindy Mediavilla were looking at two different models of participation. Mediavilla focused on the outcomes for teens who used the homework center as students. Ginny looked at outcomes for teens who worked as volunteers or paid staff in the homework centers. They speculated that the outcomes would be different in each case.

Here are some of the things that Mediavilla learned about the outcomes for teens who receive homework assistance in the library.

1. Teens realize that by participating in an after-school homework program, they are improving their study habits. They also believe that by being good students they have a positive effect on their community. Parents and homework assistance providers take an even broader view. They see the students who use the homework center as positive role models for their peers. "They're setting an example," one homework center aide said.

2. For the most part, teens feel safe studying in the library after school. This feeling of security transcends mere safety from physical danger. Not only do they feel comfortable in their surroundings, but they also feel cared for by library and homework center staff. Trust is developed between the teens and the staff over time. Students know they can go to the staff and get advice on life issues as well as homework assignments.

3. Interacting with older homework assistance providers helps teens see adults in non-classroom and non-parental roles. When the homework

helpers are volunteers, teens understand and appreciate that the adults are giving their time to help them. One mother said that it makes her daughter feel important that an engineer is tutoring her with her math.

4. Homework centers often provide space for group projects. Teens report that doing their homework in the company of their peers is more fun than doing it in isolation. Many have found that the homework center has been an arena for meeting new friends, sometimes from other schools.

5. Everyone sees the homework center as a place to learn skills that someday will be used in the workplace. This goes beyond just mastering math problems or computer skills. Parents, teachers, and library staff commented on how in the homework center the teens learn cooperation, discipline, courtesy, and problem-solving. They learn that it's okay to ask for help, and that in itself is empowering.

6. In the homework center, students learn a mode of behavior that is different from that used at home or at school. Good manners are rewarded with needed assistance. Patience is rewarded by a term on the computer or attention from the homework helper. Teamwork is encouraged or just naturally evolves.

In Ginny's study of the young people who work in public library homework programs as volunteers or as paid staff, some additional findings emerged.

1. Teen homework helpers are grateful for the opportunity to contribute to their communities. Those who have been good students themselves welcome the opportunity to help other students succeed. Teens in low-income and ethnic communities also have a keen sense of giving back to their neighborhoods. Like the students who take advantage of homework assistance programs, the teen homework helpers perceive that the educational achievement of its young people is good for the community as a whole.

2. Not many teen homework helpers see that this work enhances their own educational success. Many of them feel that they have already achieved academic success, and this is why they are working in the library. Some do find that they have become more aware of library resources as a result of their involvement with the homework center.

3. Almost all of the teen homework helpers find that working with other students and library patrons has forced them to develop new interpersonal and social skills. And like many librarians, they find parents to be more difficult to work with than their children.

4. Not all of the teen homework helpers develop meaningful relationships with the adult staff. Many are so trusted by the librarians that they are

allowed to work very autonomously. However, those who do get to know one or more of the library staff found those experiences to be especially rewarding.

5. Teens with fewer employment opportunities in their communities find that the library offers excellent training and a much more pleasant work environment than the other job opportunities available to them, such as fast food restaurants. Teens who have higher personal career expectations are more likely to see their library work experience as a resume builder or as an asset on their college applications.

6. Most teens think that the library is a safe environment. A few, who live and work in riskier inner-city environments, do not see the library as a particularly safe place. They could give examples in which dangerous incidents had occurred. However, they were realistic and said, "you're not really safe anywhere."

This ALA-sponsored research study indicates that after-school library homework assistance programs promote positive youth development in a variety of ways. Other young adult librarians whose homework centers meet the basic criteria used for this study—a designed space, a resource collection, and volunteer or paid staff providing homework assistance—could assume that their program provides similar outcomes. Or they could use the survey instrument in figure 7-2 to discover what outcomes are being delivered in their setting.

THE CHALLENGE OF EVALUATING
LIBRARY YOUTH DEVELOPMENT PROGRAMS

We have argued through much of this book that libraries should design their young adult programs according to youth development principles and practices. Youth participation is the means by which librarians can ensure that their programs develop positive developmental outcomes. And here is where a measurement dilemma occurs. We have come to equate higher numbers with higher productivity. Most library directors are eager to report higher circulation figures, higher program attendance, higher numbers of reference questions answered.

Working with young adults according to the best practice models from youth development means that we are working more intensively with fewer teens. It may be helpful to think of it as a two-tier or even a multiple-tier service model. A young adult librarian may be working closely with a group of about a dozen teens who have formed a youth advisory council. She may also be supervising a small cadre of teen workers or volunteers. This relatively small number of young adults gets a lot of attention and also presumably reaps much of the benefits of that close and sustained interaction with a responsible adult. The measurement challenge is to be able to account for and justify the greater outcomes for a smaller number, while at the same time capturing the outcomes for the larger number of teens who may be less actively involved with the library.

Here are some ways to think about this. Do the more active teens help to inform and improve library services for their peers? Do recommendations for magazine and music acquisitions from the Youth Advisory Council make the collection more relevant to other teens? Do the more active young adults actually deliver services to other teens? In the Tucson-Pima County Public Library, for example, teens are trained to give book talks at the local high school. Benefits are trickling down from the small group to a larger group of teens.

Look for ways to document and evaluate both levels of service—those to a few and those to the many.

Finally, of course, be sure to involve the teens in planning, implementing, and interpreting any evaluation strategies. Consider conducting a focus group with teens to learn what they consider to be the outcomes or benefits of a particular library program. Then brainstorm ways to develop observable or reportable indicators that those outcomes have occurred.

KNOWING SUCCESS

It is remarkable how much of our professional lives we spend just doing our jobs without thinking about whether or not we're doing the right things. We show up at the reference desk and answer questions because we are scheduled to do so. We put up posters because the bulletin board is there. We buy paperbacks for the young adult collection because the conventional wisdom tells us it's the thing to do. How often do we stop to think about the routine tasks we do or the services we provide in the overall context of what we're trying to accomplish? How would we know success if we achieved it?

Fortunately, some youth development experts have given a lot of thought to the issue of effectiveness in community-based programs for teens. The National Research Council and the Institute of Medicine have partnered and formed a Committee on Community-Level Programs for Youth. This committee reviewed all of the available research about community programs that promote positive outcomes for young adults. The result of their work is a report which was published as *Community Programs to Promote Youth Development* (Eccles and Gootman 2002). One of the most useful elements of this report is an outline of the elements that make up positive youth development settings (9–10). This forms a helpful checklist of the features in a community-based program that promote youth development and those that actually detract from it.

Nicole Yohalem and Karen Pittman (2003), from the Forum for Youth Investment, have adapted that checklist for public libraries. We see this checklist, shown here at figure 7-3, as an invaluable evaluation tool.

FIGURE 7-3 Checklist for libraries as positive settings for youth development

LIBRARIES AS POSITIVE DEVELOPMENTAL SETTINGS		
BENEFITS ZONE	**FEATURES**	**DANGER ZONE**
Physical space is safe; youth feel comfortable and welcome; building is open weekends and evenings.	**Physical and psychological safety**	Physical hazards are present; youth feel unwelcome; building hours are inconsistent.
Some spaces and activities are designed with teens' needs in mind; managed consistently with mutual respect for youth and adults.	**Appropriate structure**	Spaces and activities are too restrictive (e.g., not allowing for groups to meet, talk); activities are inconsistent, unclear, or change unexpectedly.
Designated areas are available for youth to interact with peers; youth feel supported by staff.	**Supportive relationships**	Youth do not have opportunities to interact with peers; youth feel ignored or not supported by staff.
Youth are encouraged to join groups and activities; programs, activities, and materials reflect youth interests.	**Opportunities to belong**	Youth are excluded from activities; programs, activities, and materials do not reflect youth interests.
Library staff have high expectations of youth and encourage and model positive behaviors.	**Positive social norms**	Library staff allow negative behaviors to go unaddressed or make some teens feel unwelcome, rather than helping them conform to expectations.

(Continued)

FIGURE 7-3 (Cont'd)

BENEFITS ZONE	FEATURES	DANGER ZONE
Youth-focused programs and activities are challenging and based on youth input; youth are encouraged to take active roles in the overall functioning of the library.	**Support for efficacy and mattering**	Youth input is not considered; activities are not challenging.
Staff help youth identify interests and opportunities to develop and practice skills in the library and the community.	**Opportunities for skill building**	Youth do not have opportunities to develop and practice skills in areas of interest.
Library offers opportunities for families; homework help is available; provides space for youth and community meetings and activities; works with schools.	**Integration of family, school, library, and community efforts**	Library does not offer opportunities for family activities; homework help is not available; no partnerships with schools and community organizations.
Library offers information on health and social service resources, helps assess options, may make referrals; transportation, snacks, small stipends available for special programs.	**Basic care and services**	Library is not equipped to make social service referrals; snacks, transportation never available.

This checklist provides a way for librarians to think about their services for young adults in a holistic way. Look, for example, at the third feature, "supportive relationships." We have established that supportive relationships are a positive outcome for teens. The checklist gives the librarian a framework for thinking about whether or not the library's young adult program promotes those supportive relationships. Is there a place where teens can interact with their peers? Or does the library enforce rules about quiet throughout the building? Do teens feel supported by staff? Or are they like the teens in the homework center study who were left to work alone? Are they respected as legitimate library patrons by the reference staff, or are they ignored or told that their homework problems are not legitimate questions?

THE EVALUATION COUNTER-STORY

So the counter-story about evaluation leads to accountability. It is about data as empowerment. Using data derived from good evaluation techniques, librarians have the credibility to be effective advocates for their services. Evaluation enables librarians to be accountable to decision-makers and to the teens who use their services. Evaluation transforms good intentions into results.

PART THREE

The Outsiders

Think of part 3 of this book as our response to the teens who drafted the Library Teen Bill of Rights that we presented in chapter 6. It is part of an important conversation that we continue to have with young adults. When the conversation draws to a close at the end of part 3, we will have constructed an overarching story that is a metanarrative about young adult services in public libraries. Just as metadata is data about data, our metanarrative is a narrative about narrative or a story about stories. It is a story retold from both the traditional story of the foundations of young adult library stories and the counter-stories told by new voices: the voices of youth development specialists, technology geeks, architects, teens, and sticklers for accountability.

CHAPTER 8

Making Promises to Teens

The futurists Watts Wacker and Jim Taylor talk about the promises that organizations make to their customers through their corporate images and brand names (Wacker and Taylor 2000, 52ff). We see this next installment in the story of young adult library services as being the set of promises we want to make to teens. We remember the promises that Ponyboy and his brothers made to each other and to their gang of friends in *The Outsiders*. Teens respect promises, and they expect people to keep them.

We asked teens what they wanted from public libraries. They told us. Now it is our responsibility to make some promises about what they can expect from us in return. Here are the promises we make to teens:

1. We promise to be adult professionals in all of our dealings with you.
2. We promise to be committed to your full participation in planning and implementing services intended for teens. We will work with you, not for you.
3. We promise to be engaged with the neighborhood in which you live; we will endeavor to be part of the web of primary supports for families, children, and teens in your community.
4. We promise to give you a place in the library to call your own.
5. We promise to work to ensure that the teens of tomorrow have excellent public library services. We will get it right.

Let's look briefly at each of these five promises and see what is meant by each.

WE PROMISE TO BE ADULT PROFESSIONALS
IN ALL OF OUR DEALINGS WITH YOU

We once heard David Carter, then the head of the Internet Public Library, speak to a group of young adult librarians. David is a young man, young enough to be a genuine citizen of the digital nation. But he reminded us of the danger of trying to be seen as "cool." "Let's face it," he said. "We're not cool. Most of us were *never* cool." We fail in our dealings with teens when we try to be cool or to act like them. We can, however, work with teens to create cool libraries.

Being adult professionals means that we will provide the structures and boundaries in which teens can develop. We will give directions and advice based on our experience, but we will not be rigid or prescriptive. We will provide teens with skills and opportunities to achieve the positive developmental outcomes discussed in chapter 3. We will respect young adults and have high expectations for what they can accomplish. We will not treat them like children or like fully grown adults. We will always be professional in our interactions with them. We don't need to wear ourselves out trying to be good disciplinarians and exemplary role models. Elaine has found that the staff for the Phoenix Public Library's Teen Central do well with just two guiding principles: keep it safe and keep the teens on task.

We will not whine.

We will always be grownups. Being grownups all the time means that we will exercise patience and self-control. We will make sacrifices when necessary for the welfare of the young people. We will always remember that one of the classic criteria for evaluating policy decisions is how those decisions will affect the next generation.

Being adult professionals also has implications for the role we will play in our organizations. We will be as responsible in our dealings with our library colleagues as we are with our teen customers. We will remember that the first requirement for being respected in the organization is to do good work. We will ensure that the people working with teens are the most respected employees in the library.

WE PROMISE TO BE COMMITTED
TO YOUR FULL PARTICIPATION

We hope we have made the case for the importance of youth participation in all aspects of library services launched for their benefit. We'll say it one more time: work *with* teens, not *for* them. Let's review why this is so critical.

During the second decade of life, individuals need to feel that they can influence the world around them. The only way they can accomplish this is by actually doing things that make a difference in that world. They need to see that they are important members of their communities. As we have shown, teens do have a lot they can contribute to their communities. They simply lack opportunities. Libraries can provide opportunities for meaningful participation.

It is a classic win-win situation. Young adults who work for the library, whether as volunteers or paid employees, gain skills and confidence and the sure knowledge that they are making a contribution to their community. The library in return gets the benefit of their labor, their enthusiasm and energy, and their unique insight into making the place cool. The community receives all the benefits of a well-run, vibrant library and a future return on its investment when the healthy teens of today become the productive citizens of tomorrow.

We have some strategies for keeping this promise. We will start by keeping positive youth outcomes at the forefront of our thinking about young adult library services. We will remember that not every task requires full participation; some are too menial and some are too professional for delegation to teens. We will, however, look for opportunities for meaningful teen participation; and we will make sure that young adults receive adequate training to perform the tasks assigned to them.

WE PROMISE TO BE ENGAGED
WITH YOUR NEIGHBORHOOD

We promise to make the library an important part of your community. We will get to know the other adults who work with teens—teachers, ministers, social workers, health professionals, recreation leaders, coaches, law enforcement personnel, youth advocates, and more. We will learn the community's agenda for young people and help to accomplish it. If there is no agenda for youth, we will take the initiative to develop one. We will create partnerships and generate resources to make life better for you while you are young.

We will not be content to advocate for your welfare. We will be activists and doers. We will make things happen in the library and in the community that will support you as you move through your teen years.

We will make the public library an integral and important node on the web of primary community supports for youth and families.

WE PROMISE TO GIVE YOU A PLACE OF YOUR OWN

We promise to lobby for designated teen space in the library. We will think in terms of square footage rather than shelf space, giving teens an ample field within the library. We will remember that a READ poster on the wall does not a teen place make.

We promise to listen to you throughout the planning process and to connect you with the architects and designers who will turn your ideas and ours into bricks and mortar. We will ensure that the building experts hear your visions and our professional concerns, and then we will honor their expertise. We will not try to be amateur architects and interior designers.

We promise to remember that what is cool for teens today will look as dated as yesterday's newspapers tomorrow. Today's hot topic is tomorrow's deep freeze. We will check in with you about the colors, furnishings, and equipment in the library's teen place as regularly as we ask you about your preferences in music, books, magazines, and services. We will remember how strongly you feel about quality in your environment and will keep your library space fresh, clean, and up-to-date.

WE PROMISE TO GET IT RIGHT
FOR THE TEENS OF TOMORROW

We promise to remember the discontinuity of previous library services for young adults and to work for a more sustainable future. We will be institution-builders, working to ensure that libraries will continue to get it right for coming generations of teens.

In order to accomplish this, we promise to hone our organizational skills. We will master the skills of evaluation in order to document our effectiveness and to learn from our mistakes. We will refresh our leadership and professional skills through a range of continuing education and training options. We will not burn out. We promise that the public library will be there for you—and your children and grandchildren.

In the next and final narrative chapter in this book, we will construct a story from the inside out. This is our metanarrative, the story about stories, that we want to leave with you.

CHAPTER 9

Inside Out

Last Words

Remember the voices from within the library community that you heard in the early chapters of this book. Those voices came from an honor roll of advocates and activists for young adult library services. Operating with a vision that was largely grounded in a passion for connecting teens with books, these library leaders were protagonists in a narrative that moved in fits and starts. They told a story of a small band of librarians pushing the rock of young adult services up the mountain of establishment indifference. This story of then and now is both a priceless legacy and the burden we carry into the future.

Listen once again to the new voices you heard rumbling in part 2, telling counter-stories that both enhanced and clashed with the first narrative. They talked about youth development, urging us to put the young adult before the literature or the services or the library itself. They were the voices of bits and bytes, reminding us that the teens we know today are citizens of a digital nation, a nation in which we adults are not fully enfranchised. They were the voices of teens telling us, even when we didn't ask, that they needed room to grow, places of their own in library buildings that literally marginalized them and made them feel unwelcome. We also listened to the stories architects tell when they think about creating beautiful, functional spaces. The teens spoke up again and reminded us that they are capable of articulating their own wants and needs. They told us that they can speak for themselves, given minimal training and maximum opportunities. Finally, we listened to our own left brains telling us that creativity is not enough. We heard that in order to be effective, we need to be accountable to taxpayers and government officials as well as to the teens. We need to document our story in order to tell it well.

In part 3, we invoked S. E. Hinton's novel *The Outsiders* to tell a story of promises made to the teens of today and the teens of tomorrow. This story, synthesized from the insiders and outsiders of the young adult story, is our metanarrative. In keeping with the tensions and ambiguities of our postmodern age, we see it as a story of constancy and change, durability and flexibility, empowerment and sacrifice. It is a story about partnerships between the old and the young, the library and the community, insiders and outsiders.

Ultimately, the metanarrative of young adult library services needs to be told from the inside out and from the outside in. Librarians, working inside the public library institution, must speak with the clarity and power of Margaret Edwards to update the story she told in the 1950s and 1960s. They must increasingly shift their gaze from the libraries in which they work to the communities in which their customers live. We all need to encourage outsiders from other fields and organizations to join their voices with ours. What can they tell us that will help us get it right for teens and libraries? Finally, of course, we must bring the teens inside and make them feel at home in the haven we call the library. It can be their shelter in the storm of adolescence if we choose to make it so.

We want to give a teen the last words in our book. He is a fictional teen. Ponyboy, the young protagonist of *The Outsiders,* has had a wrenching week in which a brother and a friend were lost to the violence of their mean streets. He realizes that what has happened wasn't just a personal thing to him anymore. He tells us: "Someone should tell their side of the story, and maybe people would understand then and wouldn't be so quick to judge a boy by the amount of hair oil he wore. It was important to me" (Hinton 1966, 178). After calling his English teacher to confirm that the next assigned theme can be as long as he wants, he picks up his pen and remembers the boys who had fallen. "One week had taken all of them. And I decided *I* could tell people, beginning with my English teacher" (179).

PART FOUR

Toolkit

From the beginning of our work on this book, we have planned what Margaret Edwards referred to as "A Practical Appendix." As Edwards penned in her conclusion to *The Fair Garden and the Swarm of Beasts,* "While chapters in the body of this book deal with the aims and goals of work with young adults, this appendix contains tools, i.e., instructions, lists and suggestions" (Edwards 1974, 143). As our book outline continued to change with our research, new findings in the PLPYD work, and in our personal conversations and reflections, we never wavered in our commitment to a practical section or toolkit.

While we shaped our story, counter-story, and meta-narrative, the practical tools generated during the Public Libraries as Partners in Youth Development project's four years proliferated. It soon became obvious to the Urban Libraries Council and the authors that a substantial toolkit could be easily created from tools crafted exclusively from the PLPYD project. Under the able editorial guidance of Kurstin Finch Gnehm, PLPYD tools were assembled and published in October 2002 as *Youth Development and Public Libraries: Tools for Success.* This volume provides over ninety tools for interviewing teens, training staff for work with teens, employing teens, and services with teens.

This excellent and comprehensive toolkit is available in print and CD format for a nominal fee from the Urban Libraries Council at www.urbanlibraries.org.

With this resource currently available, we decided not to duplicate any tools in the Urban Libraries Council's work. Instead, we carefully honed a few tools focused on youth participation. Beginning with the "Moderated Teen Panel," we explore the value of teen participation in staff training and provide guidance on how to prepare teen panelists, conduct the staff training, and provide follow-up staff reflection. Building on the knowledge that teens have valuable information as demonstrated in the teen panel, we provide another tool, "Youth Participation Worksheet," to enable librarians to analyze their work and identify sectors for enhanced youth participation. "Teen Voices beyond the Sound Bite" is a plea for libraries to create expanded opportunities for teens to record the impact of library participation on their lives. Last, "The World Café Process and the Library Teen Bill of Rights" documents the process used for enhancing conversation with teens and capturing teen thought as we create library practices and policy. We conclude our practical section with a short list of current resources to enable us to "get it right" as we create a lasting place for teen services in public libraries.

Moderated Teen Panel

The purpose of the moderated teen panel is to provide a venue for library staff to talk with teens. This discussion format has been one of the most powerful tools for motivating staff to rethink their commitment to teen services and teen participation in developing library programs and services. We believe this process can be adapted to a variety of staff training needs.

The moderated teen panel addresses the following goals:

1. Enable adult staff to see the unique personalities of teens and to challenge stereotypes of "all teens"
2. Motivate adult staff to work effectively with teens as customers at the reference and circulation desk and as employees
3. Provide skill-building in public speaking for teens
4. Inform library staff of the quality of teens already working with and for the library
5. Showcase the many roles played by teens in public library service

The moderated teen panel ordinarily consists of three separate activities:

- Selection and preparation of the teen panel
- Moderated teen panel staff-training session
- Follow-up session with staff

ACTIVITY ONE:
SELECTION AND PREPARATION OF TEEN PANEL

1. Select students for panel who have some experience and interest in the public library. These might include those serving as paid pages or library vol-

unteers, teens working with special programs, members of library youth councils, regular library users, etc.

2. Ask students to prepare a brief self-introduction that includes their name, age, school, neighborhood library, and how they are involved with the library. Also ask them to say something about themselves that they are very proud of and something that most people might not know about them.

3. Review commitments for students who participate. Students must prepare the self-introduction outlined in step 2. They must attend two sessions. The first session allows teens to get know each other and to review questions a day or two before the actual presentation. The second session is the actual moderated panel with adult library staff. The time for each of these meetings should be about an hour and a half.

4. Conduct preparation session with teens. This session provides time for teens to get to know the moderator and each other. Session 1 activities include:

> Adult moderator introduces him/herself to group and discusses the importance of youths' role in improving library service for teens by creating new understanding and motivation in adults who work in libraries. Moderator may use the same introduction format used by students—name, age, neighborhood library, how you are involved with the library, something about yourself that you are very proud of, and something that most people might not know about you.

> Students introduce themselves to the group using the prepared statements. This allows the moderator to have a sense of who is comfortable with speaking and who has prepared for the session. This is a good time to stress the importance of being well prepared before speaking to adult audiences.

> Go over the set of questions that you will be posing to the teens at the adult training session. Have a printed copy of the moderator's questions for teens who wish to take them home. Stress that teens should not prepare written answers to the questions. The panel answers should have a feel of spontaneity. (A suggested set of questions is found in the "Script: Moderated Teen Panel" section below.)

> Discuss the need for students to be role models and explain that some adults might ask poor questions or even be rude. Explain that if this does occur, it is the moderator's role to address poor audience behavior. Explain that students should always exhibit the respect they want to receive—in spite of what adults might do.

End by saying that the most important service youth can provide is to be honest with adults, keeping in mind that teens and adults share the goal of excellent library service for all teens.

Ask the group if they have questions or concerns about the process. They might ask about what to wear. Encourage the group to reach a consensus on this. Many teens prefer to wear their usual casual clothes. Others feel more comfortable if they are a little dressed up when they take on public speaking roles. Be sure that the students understand how questions will be monitored and how people will be selected to answer the questions.

Explain the room and audio arrangements for the panel—long table with students facing the group, microphones, name tents, etc. If possible, show students the area for the program.

ACTIVITY TWO: MODERATED TEEN PANEL STAFF-TRAINING SESSION

Room Setup: Long tables on stage area or at the front of a meeting room. Make sure the audience does not face into a distracting background behind the teen panel. Provide microphones if necessary and make sure teens practice with mikes before the program. Provide name tents for each teen panelist. Have a podium for the moderator or have the moderator with a floor mike to the side of the panel. We do not recommend the moderator joining the teens on the stage. We want the audience to focus on listening to the teens. Have a floor mike set up for the question-and-answer session that follows the panel discussion.

Time: The time provided for this activity is one and a half hours. The moderator will ask questions in the order suggested by the following script. If the teens are very articulate, you may not be able to answer all of the questions given above in ninety minutes. The moderator should decide before the panel which questions will be eliminated in the interest of time.

Record of Session: Set up a means to record this session. We suggest assigning staff to transcribe the session as it takes place. We have provided a transcript of a session done in the summer of 2001 in a California high school as an example of the need to capture this rich conversation.

Script: Moderated Teen Panel

INTRODUCTIONS

Moderator: "Good morning/afternoon. It is a pleasure to moderate today's discussion with staff and teen representatives. I would like to begin by introducing myself . . . (short introduction). I invite our teen panelists to introduce themselves." (Teens deliver prepared self-introductions practiced in first session with moderator.)

"As you can see, we have a panel that shares our commitment to our library system."

"The purpose of today's panel discussion and the following question-and-answer session is to create an accurate picture of our teen customers, volunteers, and employees. We will also discuss the nature and quality of the services that teens expect from the public library. Our goal is to increase understanding and improve services and opportunities for this valuable customer group. Our questions are grouped to cover four areas—youth and their community, library use and barriers to use, youth contributions to library and community, and strategies for making the library a more teen-friendly place."

YOUTH AND COMMUNITY

Moderator: "Our first set of questions is designed to explore the nature of the relationship between teens and adults in their families and community. We believe that youth grow up in communities, not exclusively in one family, one school, or a specific program. We want to paint a picture of what it is like to be a teen in our community in the beginning of the twenty-first century. We pose three questions to help us paint this picture of relationships and community resources."

Moderator poses one question at a time and summarizes ideas after teens answer the question. The typical answers reveal that teens want adults to respect them, set standards for them, provide safe environments, and take time to listen and to guide them. This is usually an amazing insight for adults who believe teens don't want standards or adult involvement in their lives.

1. How do you know an adult cares about you?
2. What are three things teenagers need in order to succeed at home, at school, and in the neighborhood?
3. What is the most difficult thing about being a teenager?

LIBRARY USE AND BARRIERS

Moderator: "Our next set of questions will enable us to learn more about how teens use our libraries. Some questions will help us discover any barriers teens meet when using our library. Our first questions will focus on each participant's personal use of their libraries."

1. How do you use the library? Tell us all the different things you do in any order of importance.
2. Of all the things you mentioned about using the library, what is the most important use? What is the one thing you would work the hardest to keep if the library had to reduce its services?
3. Do your friends use the library the same way that you do? Explain.
4. What do you think is the most important use of the library for your friends?
5. Why might a teen not use the library? What makes it hard about using the library?

UNDERSTANDING HOW YOUTH CONTRIBUTE TO THE LIBRARY AND COMMUNITY

Moderator: "All of you work for the library in some way. My next set of questions is about your work."

1. How do you explain your work with the library to your friends?
2. Why is your job an important one? What difference are you making? What are you learning?
3. If you could change one thing about your job, what would it be?

MAKING THE LIBRARY A MORE TEEN-FRIENDLY PLACE

Moderator: "As you know, the continued success of (name library or library service teens are involved in) is due in large part to the contributions of you and your peers. I have a few questions about how libraries can continue to improve."

1. If you could change one thing about your local library, what would it be?
2. Any ideas about library services that could be improved for teens?

PANEL CLOSING AND QUESTION-AND-ANSWER SESSION

Moderator: "I would like to thank our teen panelists for their candor and the valuable insights they have provided for us." (Let audience applaud.)

"It is now time for our question-and-answer session. We have allowed fifteen minutes for this portion of our training. We encourage you to come to the floor mike with your questions. I would like to remind our audience that this is a time for us to gather additional information, not a time to challenge teens on their opinions. Please frame questions so that opinions or statements can be clarified, not challenged. Teens, feel free to jump in with your answer. Ideally, I would like at least two teens to respond to each question.

"I will moderate this session as needed, and both the teens and I will ask for clarification of questions if needed. First question . . ."

Question-and-answer session takes place.

"I would like to close this session by again thanking our teen panelists.

"Lastly, I would like to remind staff that we will provide a transcript of this session in preparation for our next meeting to discuss what we have learned today and how to apply this learning to improving our current policies and practices.

"Thank you all."

ACTIVITY THREE:
FOLLOW-UP SESSION WITH PARTICIPATING STAFF

Establish a date and location for this follow-up session and contact all participants immediately following the panel session. Provide staff with a transcript of the panel and let them know that your meeting agenda will be a discussion of the following four questions:

1. What surprised you the most about the teens?
2. What did you learn from the teens that you didn't know before?
3. In what ways are these teens similar to and different from you when you were a teen?
4. What can the library do to make it a more teen-friendly place?

Follow-up sessions can be done locally and do not necessitate the whole group reconvening. Written results of follow-up sessions should be forwarded to appropriate administrative and training staff to determine effectiveness of the training. Next steps should also be identified.

TRANSCRIPT OF MODERATED TEEN PANEL

The following transcript documents a panel conducted with Los Angeles high school students in August 2001. The transcript was compiled from notes kept by UCLA graduate students who observed the panel presentation.

Student Profiles: All students were involved in a library instruction class for summer school credit and from a low-income, predominantly African-American community. Each student is captured by details provided in their self-introduction.

Kristen: age 14, works in school library, and school library is the library she uses most.

Ronnell: age 18, works in school library and volunteers at a nearby park.

Cassandra: age 15, uses the Westchester Branch Library of the LAPL.

Ruth: age 17, proud of her grades, uses the Westchester Branch, is involved in the USC "medcore" program and is focused on psychology.

David: age 16, uses the Inglewood Public Library, is interested in psychology.

Jose: age 14, one of 8 kids, proud of his mom who is a nurse, from Canada.

Sophia: age 17, accepted to LMU and Harvard, leaning toward LMU, is planning to be a defense lawyer, plays the violin well enough to travel the country performing.

Rick: age 17, football player, potential future librarian, bilingual, Westchester branch.

How do you know an adult cares about you?

- tells you not to do something that is wrong/ David: "Scolding is good because it means that the adult cares enough about you to bother to scold you"
- listens to you, cares about what you have to say and discusses problems with you
- asks questions like "How was your day" and is sincere/ Cassandra: "They talk to you for real"/ Jose: "They ask you how your day went and help you with your homework"
- does things for you out of the blue/ Sophia: "They might get you a gift or surprise out of the blue just because they were thinking of you during their day"
- checks up on you at school/ Ronnell: "They check in with you"

What are three things that you need to succeed at home, in school, and in the community?

- positive adults around you/ David: "positive adults around you and in your life to keep you out of trouble . . . people with time for you"
- communication, respect, and listen/ Kristen: "communication, ask questions, respect for others"/ Ruth: "listening skills: pay attention to what others say, communicate, respect, and listen"

- trust/ Jose: "Trust is necessary to gain all of the above/what everybody else said"
- Sophia: "education"

What is the most difficult thing about being a teenager?

- peer pressure/ Sophia: "peer pressure: wanting/needing to impress others"
- adults don't want to give you respect: they make unfair and incorrect assumptions about you and don't say that they are sorry when they realize they are wrong/ David: "adults: the attitudes of adults: adults don't apologize when they are frequently wrong"
- school, parental, and societal expectations: go to college, get good grades/ Ruth: "school, friends, parents, society, *pressure* from all sides and conflicting messages"
- everyone gives you mixed messages
- lack of support and trust from parents
- people don't have respect/ Ronnell: "lack of respect"
- there is too much responsibility, don't always want to do what is expected (e.g., chores)
- Cassandra: "parent's bad attitudes and lack of trust"
- Kristen: "responsibility, getting in trouble; wanting responsibility, but not chores"

How do you use the library? Tell us the different things you do in any order of importance.

- personal use (entertainment)
- read books
- multiple use/ Kristen: "for class research and homework because quiet and able to concentrate"/ Cassandra: "for a report or research paper: for school, also for recreational reading and personal study"/ Ruth: "project research, also recreational reading, time to self: quiet: nice to sit"
- a quiet place for homework
- computer access/ Sophia: "for the computer"
- a place to go when you feel bad, quiet (sanctuary?)
- to get away/ Sophia: "free quiet space, easy, relaxed"
- socializing

Of all the things you mentioned about using the library, what is the most important use—the one thing you would work the hardest to keep if the library had to reduce its service?

- Internet, because it is quicker and easier to use to find information
- books
- reference books, because teachers say you need it
- librarian (appreciation for their school librarian, who was one of the graduate students observing the panel, is apparent)
- two students begin heated discussion of Internet vs. books based on one's assertion that the Internet has updated information and the other's claim that the Internet is unreliable
- Do your friends use the library the same way that you do? Explain.
- no, they use it to talk or for computers/ Kristen: "They come to the library to talk or use the Internet"
- yes, they use it for reports or to socialize or read
- no, they don't want to take the time to use it/ Sophia: "Peers don't go to the library, or if they do they go for the computers because of their popularity and hype . . . Peers have better things to do, or different priorities that don't include library use, such as not highly interested in good grades, therefore they don't see library as a resource for academic support"
- consensus on the question of what the most important use of the library is for friends: educational support

Why might a teen not use the library? What makes it hard about using the library? Barriers to teen library use:

- some teens are afraid to ask questions/ Sophia: "Teens are afraid to ask questions: afraid to let somebody know that they don't know everything: pride, ego . . . also afraid of what friends might think of them (as a nerd)": lots of agreement on this point
- the order is confusing (e.g., the card catalog)/ Cassandra: "How to find books? confusingly organized? difficult system for first-time users to learn/access": lots of teens chimed in agreement on this point
- Jose: "understanding how to use the library . . . the library's system of organization . . . impatience of librarians . . . their not showing patrons to the stacks to help locate their book/item"
- "the way that librarians or library staff treat teens where the first thing out of their mouth can be detrimental to future visits or questions, librarians should be eminently approachable"

- librarians think teens already know how to use library (stems from librarians unhappy with job and not wanting to adequately serve patrons)
- teens are lazy and would rather use Barnes & Noble/ Rick: "Teens don't use the library out of laziness . . . computer is easier, else Barnes & Noble . . . also problems with asking for help and problems with the librarians supposed to give/provide assistance"
- teens are intimidated by books and the library
- teens don't like the way it looks
- the lighting is dull, need more light shining in
- dusty books
- library needs some color (discussion about painting the Westchester High School library)
- (Library layout and design spark conversation about Teen'Scape—I am surprised almost all the students don't know about it. Also, there is some discussion about Barnes & Noble and the comfortable sofas, making the environment a place to relax.)

How would you design a library? Specific comments on Westchester High School Library:

- more computers
- more color
- lively books (not the dated books from the 1980s—I laugh to myself, feeling old)
- use pictures and words to identify sections as an alternative to confusing classification system
- make it a more social environment with couches and pictures
- Internet on all computers
- too dusty now, change the environment
- put the encyclopedias somewhere besides the front of the library to establish a welcoming entrance
- put magazines, couches, and books that kids like at the front so atmosphere is more relaxed
- put in plants and lights (Christmas lights anyone?)

General comments on how library service to teens could be improved:

- books organized better (or more obviously) to make finding easier

- improved signage to encourage self-help
- Internet on all computers
- cleaner
- general environment: lighting, furniture, etc.
- allow eating in library
- round tables
- not seeing the encyclopedias first thing as you walk into the library
- couches
- more magazines, popular reading
- more natural light
- couches, relaxation-supportive areas
- more hired help with knowledge of the collection
- hire helpful people with positive personal attitudes
- hire enthusiastic and caring adults
- to avoid ageism and age discrimination, students/teens could be on the interview panel to select new library personnel
- Cassandra: "All the decisions adults make affect kids, but kids aren't involved in the decision-making process (this frustrates teens)"

Why is your job at the library an important one? And what difference are you making through this work?

- Cassandra: "help (librarian) . . . help other students . . . learn how the library operates . . . helping"
- Ruth: "help others . . . interact with others . . . readers' advisory"
- Kristen: "communication skills . . . helping people . . . helping kids with school work"
- David: "computers . . . (helping people use computers) . . . also bettering his own education through library work"
- Jose: "show people computers . . . Encarta encyclopedia . . . mouse instruction . . . teaching basic computer skills (that others will need to succeed) . . . basic computer instruction is key to their (the people he helps/instructs) future"
- Rick: "help people find books for reports . . . keeping track of books"
- If you could change one thing about your job, what would it be?
- more variety

- job allocation based on skills assessment/inventory
- add music to library setting

Would you become a librarian? What would you need to make becoming a librarian more attractive?

- pay for education
- Internet
- work with kids
- help people
- change peoples' lives

Youth Participation Worksheet

The purpose of the youth participation worksheet is to enable staff to create new opportunities for teens to participate in the work of public libraries. This activity exemplifies a process used by libraries in the PLPYD initiative to explore ways to provide the necessary supports (things done *with* teens) and opportunities (activities, roles, and responsibilities performed *by* teens) for teens to participate.

We suggest a six-step process that can be applied to any library activity in which teens may wish to participate. The steps are as follows:

1. List the steps necessary for the task to be completed.
2. Designate which of the steps would be appropriate for teen participation. Check this recommendation with teens.
3. Define the outcomes for teens who participate.
4. List the supports needed for teens.
5. List the opportunities for teens.
6. Create an evaluation of your process in the achievement of youth outcomes.

Once you have created this model using a blank worksheet, create a timeline, gather resources, discuss the plan with all adult staff that will be impacted by the new program, make modifications based on their suggestions, and last, review the process with teens who will be involved. We have provided a suggested model for teen participation in collection development, followed by a blank worksheet.

MODEL FOR YOUTH PARTICIPATION
IN COLLECTION DEVELOPMENT

Step One: List steps for collection development of teen materials.

- Create a collection development statement and user profile.
- Establish a process for reviewing materials.
- Order, purchase, and prepare materials for the collection.
- Display and promote materials.
- Evaluate user satisfaction.

Step Two: Designate which step/s are best suited for teen participation. Check with teens.

- We recommend the "display and promote materials" step for teen participation

Step Three: Define outcomes for youth who participate.

- Meaningful relationships with adults and teens
- Marketable skills of program management, evaluation, and marketing
- Educational success in fulfilling required community service hours

Step Four: List supports or what you will do with teens. Staff and teens will:

- Enlist local merchants to provide training in marketing and displays.
- Use local university staff or students to help teens design focus groups or online surveys to determine materials and topics of interest to community teens.
- Use the Search Institute's booklet *Step by Step: A Young Person's Guide to Positive Community Change* (Search Institute 2001) and have staff work with teens in program management.
- Tour acquisitions department to learn how materials are selected, ordered, and processed.
- Designate adult mentor/s to work with teens for questions and to make sure teen outcomes are met and documented.

Step Five: List opportunities or work that will be done by teens independently. Teens will:

- Decide on topics/themes for display based on research.
- Define tasks that are the sole responsibility of teens and create strategy for completing tasks and reporting progress.

- Plan physical layout of display and create means for maintaining display.
- Create a method for determining success of the display and report on success to appropriate stakeholders.

Step Six: Create an evaluation of your process based on youth outcomes.

- Teens will submit work log of skills mastered and goals met.
- Teens will complete a survey on their relationship with their adult mentor.
- Teens will submit time sheets for community service hours completed.

*Youth Participation in*_____ *Worksheet*

Step One: List steps for _____

- _____
- _____
- _____

Step Two: Designate which step/s are best suited for teen participation. Check with teens.

- _____
- _____
- _____

Step Three: Define outcomes for youth who participate.

- _____
- _____
- _____

Step Four: List supports or what you will do with teens. Staff and teens will:

- _____
- _____
- _____

Step Five: List opportunities or work that will be done by teens independently. Teens will:

- _____
- _____
- _____

Step Six: Create an evaluation of your process based on youth outcomes.

- _____
- _____
- _____

Teen Voices beyond the Sound Bite

The purpose of this section is to give a fuller voice to teens in public libraries. We have discussed the role of teens in creating book reviews and other print or website postings. We would like to challenge libraries to create venues for expanded teen voices that capture the nature, impact, and value of participation in public libraries. We offer the following example to make our case for expanded participation created by richer writing opportunities.

A DAY IN THE LIFE OF A TEEN LIBRARY WORKER:
Five Hours in the World of a Teen Library Worker
Courtesy of the 2000–2001 Youth Partnership Council
by Dominica Clark

This is a day in the life of a teen library worker. This doesn't mean these events will occur to you, but this is the writer's true experience. So this Journal Diary is a personal piece in the sense that it is not just dry information but prose, mind you. In no way will the author give views on politics or say anything that may be deemed offensive, though the author would like to have a few words in for politics, but that's entirely off the subject! And thus, I give you, "A Day in the Life of a Teen Library Worker"!

Pre-Arrival: My day in the library starts as school comes to an end. My last class is mass media and it usually leaves me in an inspirational mood. I am looking forward to work. So Liz and I leave school. By now it's a little after 3 o'clock and I need to be at work at 4:00, so there's just enough time to stop by a certain store.

So we purchase some items and drive to the library with Death Cab for Cutie cranked up, and as we are heading to the actual library I start thinking about how lucky I am to have this job at the Auburn Library (which is part of the King County Library System) in Seattle, Wash. (No! I was really thinking that!)

I have done nearly everything librarians would typically do (all limited and to a certain extent, though). This is a job that enables me to use my creativity, and judgment, and it makes me deal with stress and problems and it's wonderful, because this isn't any ordinary passive, monotonous job. I'm helping people.

4:00: The Arrival: For the first 15 minutes, I do things related to getting ready to work. I check my e-mail on the interlibrary account for the King County Library System, I check my box (yes! I get a box!) and I put things away in the locker that I share with a fellow teen worker. I look for the stuff I put on hold; in particular, I put a hold on the Velvet Underground album, which arrived that day. I peek out of the hole that leads to the main library area. The library is abuzz with activities and the reference desk is swarmed with patrons. I go to Bonnie's desk (the young adult librarian) to work out my schedule for January. By the way, on the subject of staff, I don't know if it's just this library but every single one (every one!) of my coworkers is intellectual and incredibly interesting, so it's great to work with such personalities.

After working out my schedule, I am told to clean the children's section, which is my favorite. As usual, it is made up of scattered regular picture books and baby books. Crumpled papers and pencils lay on the floor and the puzzles available to kids lay untouched, thank goodness. It may seem like a drag to clean up the children's area, but no! It feels good being in that area, surrounded by children's books and a child's mess and to hear their whispering in the distance . . . (behind the Easy Non-Fiction Section).

After that is done, I say, ah, what the heck, I'll do some more cleaning (don't tell Bonnie or Fran!) and I straighten books and obsessively put things in right order and pick up every odd crumb. After that (about 40 minutes have gone by), I clean the young adult area, which is now inhabited by a guy sitting on the couch/chairs, reading the *Auburn Reporter,* and a bunch of people at a round table, talking. Not much to do here.

I go to the reference desk and help out Bonnie and Terry for about an hour, a little less. It's relatively slow today, so we take it easy, and I help people get signed up for the Internet. I love looking at all these people, gathered and passing, and once in a while, I end up, indirectly, helping people with reference questions, which I'm not supposed to do. Then, I wash the privacy screens, which is a lot more fun than it sounds, at the reference desk.

At this point, Bonnie says she has a project for me to do, and it's a good one, trust me. Processing books is the bomb, I love books and I am constantly snooping through the "new book" pile and I love books generally, so it's great fun. I sit for about thirty minutes in the back room with people passing me by, my music on low (I heard Make-up for the first time today!) and it's great! First, the possession stamp on the outside, inside on the first page. Then the "aubu" sticker on the bottom right-hand side. Then (here's the fun part), the processing paper with the bar code on it (I forget the name!), and then putting a soft, sticky thing over it to protect it.

6:30 pm: So the day at the Auburn Library is halfway over and that means my break, which I'm a little thankful for. The break room, as it is, is very comfortable and soft and pleasing, and especially so when the fluorescent lights are not blaring. I listen to the Velvet Underground record and munch, munch on Fig Newtons and orange juice.

I return after my ten-minute break and Bonnie finds me. I am assigned a tedious, long job but probably one of the most pleasurable I've had yet. Books that are "lost" or supposedly, are put on "trace" in the system. It is my job to find those books and see if they are on the shelves and if they are, to bring them back, if not, well, I shall think of them, out there somewhere in the world. That takes about an hour and a half, a little more. I love it! Along the way, I get asked questions and point people in the right direction, a young girl asks me for a book on horses, about 15 minutes are diverted to help her.

Along the way, with my red cart, I find, as usual when the shelving and the like, books I want for myself, adding to the cart around twenty things I have already checked out. I end up cleaning a lot along the way, picking up stray papers and recycling them.

8:00: By this time, the library has really slowed down and for a while, realizing how much I've been doing, shelving-kind of work, Bonnie lets me help at the reference desk for a while. With working at the reference desk, you help people with everything and anything. In my job I am actually allowed to work at the reference desk, where you would need to get a Master's in Library Science and I am actually allowed to be behind the desk, and I especially love being there. You watch people come and go and you help people who really need it, and you're around these people of all sorts, and I love helping and searching and dealing, it's all quite exhilarating.

Then Bonnie tries to find something else for me to do, so I tell her I'll shelve. So I shelve, and let my mind wander and I put away two full carts of adult fiction and children's books, which is, though a wee bit tiring, also lotsa fun.

By this time it is five minutes to closing and me and Liz scramble around and turn off computers, while she hits me with rubber bands and I try to get her but end up hitting Judy instead (who's also a circulation desk worker). Judy is way cool, so she's not angry or anything. I go in the main area one last time to, with my own will, straighten chairs and straighten things up generally. Liz spots me and we head to the back and get ready to leave, we check out numerous things at the circulation desk and say good-bye to Bonnie, who's doing something at the desk in the deserted library. Lights are turned off, laughing is heard in the back room and me and Liz walk out into the cold, dark night, and thus, my friends, a day in the life of a teen librarian.

The World Café Process and the Library Teen Bill of Rights

The purpose of this section is to provide details of the process described in chapter 6, "Conversation: The Power of Teen Voices." While specific to the creation of the Library Teen Bill of Rights, this process can be adapted to any conversation that you would want to have with a group of teens.

The World Café process is founded on the belief that most of the talent and knowledge for any task exist within the group assembled for a conversation about the task. The inspiration comes from creating an atmosphere that combines comfort, playfulness, and the stimulation of listening deeply to many people in small dynamic groups. We will present here the final background materials sent to all participants, the setup of the room for the café meeting, and the specific activities that introduce the World Café and shape the method of ever-changing conversation and refinement of thought.

BACKGROUND MATERIALS

Two weeks prior to our PLPYD Youth Partnership Council meeting, delegates were sent a packet of information for pre-reading and thinking. The materials were titled "Library Teen Bill of Rights Project" and contained the following introduction.

> On Sunday morning, July 28, Elaine Meyers will be working with the delegates to create a Library Teen Bill of Rights. The bill will be included in the book that she and Dr. Virginia Walter are writing about youth development and the public library. This is a great opportunity to incorporate teens' voices in the book. The book, which will be published by

the American Library Association, will be read by a wide audience inside and outside the library profession.

If possible, we'd like delegates and chaperones to do a little pre-conference thinking about bills of rights and what the Library Teen Bill of Rights might contain. In this packet, you have four samples of bills of rights—the U.S. Bill of Rights, the Library Bill of Rights from the American Library Association, the Youth Bill of Rights from the National Child Rights Alliance, and the Brookline Youth Lacrosse Player Bill of Rights. The third-year delegates decided that these four samples would help to get everyone thinking about the project.

Please read (and make notes) on these samples, and in the cab, or on the plane, or in the airport en route to the conference, take a moment to discuss the readings and the project with your team. We only have three hours on Sunday morning to complete the bill, so we need everyone to do some thinking and talking beforehand!

All four documents are available on the Internet. There are multiple sources for the U.S. Bill of Rights, but we found the ACLU's briefing paper to be very useful, at www.aclu.org/library/pbp9.html. The Library Bill of Rights is found at www.ala.org. The Youth Bill of Rights is available at www.parent.net/facts/archive/youthRights.html, and the Lacrosse Player Bill of Rights is at http://home.attbi.com/~scottrunnr/player Rights.html.

ROOM SETUP

Provide round café tables that seat six to eight participants. We had twenty-four delegates for our exercises, or four tables. Cover tables with paper so that participants can doodle and write ideas. Provide a variety of colored markers and crayons for participants to use. We included pipe cleaners, small Styrofoam balls and shapes, feathers, and small containers of Play Dough for sculptural "doodling." Candy dishes were at each table, and teens made great use of foil candy wrappers in creating a gallery of small sculptures. We were so surprised by the quality of the informal art that we improvised a showcase and had teens vote on the best sketches and sculptures at our final break. We had a variety of small prizes that we awarded to the prize-winning artists.

Cover the walls of your café with quotes appropriate to the process and the topic of conversation. We do not mean a few posters; we mean lots of posters within eyeshot of all participants. We covered walls and columns with multiple copies of the following slogans:

The knowledge and wisdom is already present and accessible.

Collective insight evolves from honoring unique contributions, connecting ideas, listening into the middle, noticing deeper themes and questions.

Focus on what matters.

Contribute your thinking and expertise.

Speak from the heart.

Listen to understand.

Link and connect ideas.

Listen together for deeper themes, insights, and questions.

Play, doodle, draw—writing on the tablecloths is encouraged.

"A Bill of Rights is what the people are entitled to against every government on earth, general or particular, and what no just government should refuse." —Thomas Jefferson

Rights are what no library should refuse.

Authentic Rights are easily agreed upon to be true universal Rights.

"People naturally possess certain Rights—life, liberty and property. Rulers derive their power only from the consent of the people they rule." —John Locke

Rights imply responsibilities.

How do you distinguish between a right and a "want"?

A document by teens for teens.

You are at the epicenter of the information revolution, ground zero of the digital world. You helped build it, and understand it as well or better than anyone. Not only is the digital world making you more sophisticated, altering your ideas of what culture and literacy are, it is connecting you to one another, providing you with a sense of political self. In the digital age you are neither unseen nor unheard; in fact, you are seen and heard more than ever. You occupy a new kind of cultural space. You are a citizen of a new order, founder of the Digital Nation. —Adapted from the first paragraph of Jon Katz's "The Digital Rights of Kids in the Digital Age," *Wired,* July 1996

Provide black markers and Post-it flip chart paper for each table host. The moderator must have a flip chart with the questions for each café rotation clearly written on it. Designate two adults to transcribe the notes from each table for the final question. This final question is the Library Teen Bill of Rights, and by this point the teens are slightly tired from all their thinking and talking. We had the adults not only transcribe the last session, but combine key ideas. The computer was hooked up to a projection device so that the group could view their final product and make final adjustments, as described in the last activity listed below.

ACTIVITIES

1. Introduce the topic of conversation and the task to be accomplished. In the case of the Library Teen Bill of Rights, Elaine talked about the plans for this book and our desire to showcase a unique teen contribution. She explained that at the heart of the planned book was the question, "Why have services to teens in public libraries not been as consistent as services to children?" She explained that she and Virginia have found examples of golden ages of teen services in public libraries, but no consistent trajectory toward a goal of excellent institutionalized services. She also talked about the changes technology has made in the public library and how technology has renewed many teens' use of the library. Elaine concluded by saying that she and Virginia believe that the answer to lasting change lies in the increased participation of teens in designing and implementing services. Elaine then took a moment to thank the senior leadership team who helped with the process and in the preparation of the background materials.

2. Introduce the rules of the café. The first rule is that someone at each table must volunteer to serve as the *table host*. The host's job is to stay at one table and record the group's ideas. When the table participants change, the host stays at the table to brief the new group on the first group's ideas and to make additions and corrections based on instructions from the second group. Two of the teens from the senior leadership group volunteered as table hosts, and two more of the older teens comfortable with leadership roles volunteered as hosts. The second rule is that no adults are included in the café process. They were allowed to observe from the sidelines, but could not actively participate in any discussion. The third rule is to follow the guidelines established by the moderator and to bring questions to the moderator for clarification.

3. The role of the moderator is explained as that of clarifying the questions that all tables will be discussing. The moderator has all questions written for posting and would introduce the question and tell participants to move to another table to continue their conversations.

4. The moderator posts the first questions, "What are the characteristics of a bill of rights? What do we need to know to write a bill of rights?" The moderator has hosts write the questions on a Post-it flip chart and begin to record the answers of the group at the table. The group spends five to eight minutes at the first table. Then the moderator asks the host to record the last idea. The teens are then asked to go to another table—one that does not contain anyone at the previous table. When settled (make sure that teens do go to tables with different participants), the moderator then asks the host to read the work on the first group and then have participants remove ideas or add to existing ideas. The group works for five minutes and then changes under the same procedures as the first change.

5. The moderator then calls for the hosts to post their flip-chart notes and recap the characteristics of a bill of rights. When all results are posted, the moderator calls for a short break. During our session, the posted flip charts contained the following information:

A bill of rights is

- a document with policies that civilians send to government officials regarding their wants and needs
- a document that states the rights awarded to the individuals and the responsibilities imposed upon them to ensure the security and longevity of the rights
- statements saying their freedoms within a group or organization
- to ensure the liberty of the people
- what the people thought about their freedoms
- self-expression
- rights, responsibilities, and privileges
- principles
- guarantees rights to individual people
- what people are entitled to
- rights that no government should refuse
- government non-dictatorship
- to ensure the liberty of the people in a nation
- to make a statement everyone agrees on
- rights without costs to receiving them
- freedom

- to guard and shield the people
- to feel safe
- equality to all people
- document that explains and protects the natural rights of people
- lists responsibilities, privileges, and roles of participants within a certain institution
- rights may be assessed for individual groups
- meant to prevent dictatorship in the government
- helps to guarantee that no one person or group will take these rights away and gain too much power

6. After the break, the moderator reviews the common points from the group reports on the characteristics of a bill of rights. Participants are asked to sit at new tables and work on the second question, with the table host remaining the same at each table. The second question is, "What can we learn from the ALA Bill of Rights that will help us create a Library Teen Bill of Rights?" The same procedure is followed, with only two rotations taking place. The host reviews and posts notes from each table. The following are the responses from our teens to the second question:

What can we learn from the ALA Bill of Rights?

- They don't exclude people due to race or views or any other personal circumstances
- General, but address the needs of library patrons
- All materials are available for the purposes of interest, information, and enlightenment of all people
- Are these rights recommended or guaranteed?
- Teens should not be denied access to library resources based on age or reason
- Teens should not be under constant surveillance because of age
- Teens should fight censorship to some extent
- Teens should not be denied a space in the library to call their own
- In addition to general spaces, teens should have their own designated space
- Teens should challenge censorship in the fulfillment of their responsibility to receive information and enlightenment

- A teen's right to have their own space should not be denied because of their age* or other reasons. (*Although people of all ages are *not* denied access to this space, it should be kept in mind that the space is for *teens* and when being built, this should be kept in mind!)
- Libraries should cooperate with teens concerned with resisting abridgement of free expression, assembly, and access to ideas
- All patrons are protected by article 5 of the ALA Library Bill of Rights
- The ALA set standards for us to go by and improve
- It justified participants and citizens who pass through the library
- Any service you receive from the library is free

Note the increased clarity of thought and precision of language in the second set of responses. The effect of the process on sharpening thought is evident.

7. The final assignment was not a question, but directions to create a Library Teen Bill of Rights at each table. Groups were rotated twice, and when the work was finished, charts were given to adult scribes who typed the work and consolidated similar ideas. During this final break, teens submitted their sketches and small sculptures for the group to award winners in a variety of categories—sketch, clay, and "mixed media." The artwork was as stunning as the draft of the bill. After the break, teens reviewed the draft bill and discussed the issues of parental control; rights versus wants in teen places; and control and guidelines on moving beyond sole dependence on electronic resources. The final Library Teen Bill of Rights is found in chapter 6. After the morning's work, adult observers remarked that the bill was an example of some of the finest work teens had accomplished to date. We agreed and credit their years of involvement with the library, their progressive leadership experience, and the World Café process for this success.

Further Resources

Youth development and intensive youth participation are not new to public libraries, and best practices continue to be developed and built upon. In the past five years, a number of toolkits have been developed to aid public libraries for these purposes.

American Psychological Association

A Reference for Professionals: Developing Adolescents. 2002. www.apa.org/pi/pii/develop.pdf

Chapin Hall Center for Children

A Self-Study Guide for Managers and Staff of Primary Support Programs for Young People. Joan Costello, Gary Barker, and Lisa Marie Pickens. 2000. www.chapin.uchicago.edu/ ProjectsGuide/ (see Primary Supports section for free downloadable copy)

County of Los Angeles Public Library

Teens: The Community Service Solution. Virginia Walter and Natalie Cole. 2000. www.colapublib.org/teen/

United Way of America

Measuring Program Outcomes: A Practical Approach. 1996. Item number 0989; call (800) 772-008 to order

Urban Libraries Council

Youth Development and Public Libraries: Tools for Success. Kurstin Finch Gnehm, ed. 2002.

References

"About the Michael L. Printz Award." 2002. Chicago: Young Adult Library Services Association. Available at www.ala.org/yalsa/printz/aboutaward. html. Last accessed January 4, 2003.

"The Alex Awards: Policies and Procedures." 2002. Chicago: Young Adult Library Services Association. At www.ala.org/yalsa/yalsainfo/alexinfo. html. Last accessed January 4, 2003.

American Library Association. 1999. "Way Cool: Designing Young Adult Spaces That Work." Annual Conference program. Available at www. ala.org/lama. Last accessed April 9, 2001.

Astroth, Kirk. 1994. "Beyond Ephebiphobia: Problem Adults or Problem Youths." In "Beyond Ephebiphobia: A Tool Chest for Customer Service to Young Adults." Published for the President's Program, 113th Annual Conference of the American Library Association, Miami Beach, Fla.

Beers, G. Kylene. 1996. "No Time, No Interest, No Way! The Three Voices of Aliteracy." *School Library Journal* 42 (February): 30–33.

"Beyond Ephebiphobia: A Tool Chest for Customer Service to Young Adults." 1994. Published for the President's Program, 113th Annual Conference of the American Library Association, Miami Beach, Fla.

Bilal, Dania. 2000. "Children's Use of the Yahooligans! Web Search Engine: I. Cognitive, Physical and Affective Behaviors on Fact-based Search Tasks." *Journal of the American Society for Information Science and Technology* 51 (May): 646–65.

———. 2001. "Children's Use of the Yahooligans! Web Search Engine: II. Cognitive and Physical Behaviors on Research Tasks." *Journal of the American Society for Information Science and Technology* 52 (January): 118–36.

Bishop, Kay, and Pat Bauer. 2002. "Attracting Young Adults to Public Libraries: Frances Henne/YALSA/VOYA Research Grant Results." *Journal of Youth Services in Libraries* 15 (winter): 36–44.

"BIX—The Library Index, Current Status." 2001. Available at www.bertelsmann-stiftung.du/documents/Projekt_Info_English_010112.pdf. Last accessed November 11, 2002.

Bozeman, Barry, and Jeffrey D. Straussman. 1990. *Public Management Strategies: Guidelines for Managerial Effectiveness.* San Francisco: Jossey-Bass.

Braun, Linda W. 2002. *Teens.library: Developing Internet Services for Young Adults.* Chicago: American Library Association.

Braverman, Miriam. 1979. *Youth, Society, and the Public Library.* Chicago: American Library Association.

Cahill, Michele. 1997. "Youth Development and Community Development: Promises and Challenges of Convergence." Paper presented at a meeting sponsored by the Ford Foundation and the International Youth Foundation.

Campbell, Patty. 1994. Foreword to *The Fair Garden and the Swarm of Beasts: The Library and the Young Adult,* by Margaret A. Edwards. Reprint edition. Chicago: American Library Association.

———. 1998. *Two Pioneers of Young Adult Library Services.* VOYA Occasional Papers Series. Lanham, Md.: Scarecrow.

Carter, Betty. 2002. Foreword to *The Fair Garden and the Swarm of Beasts: The Library and the Young Adult,* by Margaret A. Edwards. Centennial edition. Chicago: American Library Association.

Caywood, Caroline A., editor. 1995. *Youth Participation in School and Public Libraries: It Works.* Chicago: American Library Association.

Chelton, Mary K., editor. 1994. *Excellence in Library Services to Young Adults: The Nation's Top Programs.* Chicago: American Library Association.

Costello, Joan, Gary Barker, and Lisa Marie Pickens. 2000. *A Self-Study Guide for Managers and Staff of Primary Support Programs for Young People.* Chicago: Chapin Hall Center for Children.

———. 2001. "Promoting Public Library Partnerships with Youth Agencies." *Journal of Youth Services in Libraries* 15 (fall): 8–15.

"Developmental Assets: An Overview." N.d. Minneapolis: Search Institute. Available at http://search-institute.org/assets/. Last accessed July 5, 2001.

Donahue, Patricia L., et al. 1999. *NAEP 1998 Reading Report Card for the Nation.* Washington, D.C.: National Center for Education Statistics. Available at http:/nces.ed.gov/nationsreportcard/pubs/main1009/199459.shmtl. Last accessed January 6, 2003.

Dresang, Eliza. 1999. *Radical Change: Books for Youth in a Digital Age.* New York: H. W. Wilson.

Eccles, Jacquelynne, and Jenifer Appleton Gootman, editors. 2002. *Community Programs to Promote Youth Development.* Washington, D.C.: National Academy.

Edwards, Margaret A. 1974. *The Fair Garden and the Swarm of Beasts: The Library and the Young Adult.* Revised and expanded edition. New York: Hawthorn.

Fidel, Raya, Rachel K. Davies, Mary H. Douglass, et al. 1999. "A Visit to the Information Mall: Web Searching Behavior of High School Students." *Journal of the American Society for Information Science* 50:24–37.

Finch Gnehm, Kurstin, editor. 2002. *Youth Development and Public Libraries: Tools for Success.* Evanston, Ill.: Urban Libraries Council.

Fowler, Mathew. 2002. Written document submitted to Elaine Meyers.

Give 'Em What They Want! Managing the Public's Library. 1992. Chicago: American Library Association.

Gladwell, Malcolm. 2000. *The Tipping Point: How Little Things Can Make a Big Difference.* Boston: Little, Brown.

Hackett, John. 2000. "Banks Toy Around with Burgeoning Kids Market." *Bank Technology News* (July). Available at http://banktechnews.com/btn/articles/btnjul00-2.shtml. Last accessed November 11, 2002.

"Hennen's American Public Library Ratings." 2002. Available at http://www.haplr-index.com/fax.html. Last accessed November 11, 2002.

"Highsmith Award Description." 2002. Available at urbanlibraries.org/Highsmith%202002.html. Last accessed October 19, 2002.

Himmel, Ethel, and William James Wilson. 1998. *Planning for Results: A Public Library Transformation Process.* Chicago: American Library Association.

Hine, Thomas. 1999. *The Rise and Fall of the American Teenager.* New York: Avon.

Hinton, S. E. 1966. *The Outsiders.* New York: Viking.

———. 1971. *That Was Then, This Is Now.* New York: Delacorte.

———. 1975. *Rumble Fish.* New York: Delacorte

Jacobson, Frances F., and Emily N. Ignacio. 1997. "Teaching Reflection: Information Seeking and Evaluation in a Digital Library Environment." *Library Trends* 45 (spring): 771–99.

Jensen, Richard. 2000. *Clark and Menefee.* New York: Princeton Architectural Press.

Jones, Patrick. 2002. *New Directions for Library Service to Young Adults.* Chicago: American Library Association.

Kanter, Rosabeth Moss. 1994. "Collaborative Advantage: The Art of Alliances." *Harvard Business Review* 72 (July–August): 96–108.

Katz, Jon. 1996. "The Digital Rights of Kids in the Digital Age." *Wired* 4 (July): 120–23, 166–70.

Kretzmann, John P., and John L. McKnight. 1993. *Building Communities from the Inside Out: A Path toward Finding and Mobilizing a Community's Assets.* Chicago: AACTA Publications.

"Latest Survey Results: Teen Read Week 2002." 2002. SmartGirl.org, at http://www.smartgirl.org/reports/1493716.html. Last accessed January 6, 2003.

Leigh, Robert D. 1950. *The Public Library in the United States.* New York: Columbia University Press.

Lenhart, Amanda, Lee Rainie, and Oliver Lewis. 2001. *Teenage Life Online: The Rise of the Instant-Message Generation and the Internet's Impact on Friendships and Family Relationships.* Washington, D.C.: Pew Internet and American Life Project. Available at http://www.pewinternet.org/. Last accessed January 15, 2002.

Levin, Douglas, and Sousan Arafeh. 2002. *The Digital Disconnect: The Widening Gap between Internet-Savvy Students and Their Schools.* Washington, D.C.: Pew Internet and American Life Project. Available at www.pewinternet.org/reports/toc/asp?Report=67. Last accessed January 3, 2003.

Libbey, Heather. 1999. "Comparing, Contrasting, and Integrating Different Developmental Frameworks and Initiatives." Paper presented at

Healthy Communities, Healthy Youth Conference, Denver, Colo., November 12, 1999. Available at www.ctassets.org/pdf/reading/matrix. pdf. Last accessed February 3, 2003.

"Margaret A. Edwards Award." 2002. Chicago: Young Adult Library Services Association. Available at www.ala.org/yalsa/edwards/facts.html. Last accessed January 4, 2003.

Martin, Lowell. 1983. "The Public Library: Middle-Age Crisis or Old Age?" *Library Journal* 108 (January 1): 17–22.

McClure, Charles R., et al. 1987. *Planning and Role Setting for Public Libraries: A Manual of Options and Procedures.* Chicago: American Library Association.

McCook, Kathleen de la Peña. 2000. *A Place at the Table: Participating in Community Building.* Chicago: American Library Association.

Measuring Program Outcomes: A Practical Approach. 1996. Alexandria, Va.: United Way of America. Excerpts available at http://national.united-way.org/outcomes/intro.htm. Last accessed January 20, 2003.

Mediavilla, Cindy. 2001. *Creating the Full-Service Homework Center in Your Library.* Chicago: American Library Association.

———. 2001. "Why Library Homework Centers Extend Society's Safety Net." *American Libraries* 32, no. 12:40–42.

Meyers, Elaine. 1999. "The Coolness Factor: Ten Libraries Listen to Youth." *American Libraries* 30, no. 10:42–45.

———. 2001. "The Road to Coolness: Youth Rock the Public Library." *American Libraries* 32, no. 2:46–48.

———. 2002. Interview with architect Richard Jensen. November 12, 2002.

———. 2002. "Youth Development and Libraries: A Conversation with Karen Pittman." *Public Libraries* 41 (September-October): 256–60.

Molz, Redmond Kathleen, and Phyllis Dain. 1999. *Civic Space/Cyberspace: The American Public Library in the Information Age.* Cambridge, Mass.: MIT Press.

Moore, David W., et al. 1999. *Adolescent Literacy: A Position Statement.* International Reading Association.

Munson, Amelia H. 1950. *An Ample Field: Books and Young People.* Chicago: American Library Association.

National Training Institute for Community Youth Development Work. 2000. "Youth Development Program for Public Libraries as Partners in

Youth Development." Washington. D.C.: Academy for Educational Development.

"New Central Library I.C." 2001. Summary of remarks made by Bill Sannwald. Available at http://www.mpls.lib.mn.us/minutes/ ic032701.asp. Last accessed November 12, 2002.

Nilsen, Richard. 1995. "Building Reflects Heart of Its Architect." *Arizona Republic/Phoenix Gazette,* May 14, 1995, special section, 12.

"Ontario Public Library Guidelines." 1999. Second edition. Available at www.olsn.on.ca/Guidelines/Edition99-eng/Appendix_B_99.pdf. Last accessed November 11, 2002.

Palladino, Grace. 1996. *Teenagers: An American History.* New York: BasicBooks.

"The Phoenix Summary Budget 1998–99." 1998. Available at http://www.ci.phoenix.az.us/BUDGET/budget.html. Last accessed January 5, 2003.

Pittman, Karen. 2000. "Balancing the Equation: Communities Supporting Youth, Youth Supporting Communities." *Community Youth Development* 1 (winter): 32–36. Also available at http://www.cydjournal.org/ 2000Winter.Pittman.html. Last accessed February 3, 2003.

Public Library Association. Goals, Guidelines, and Standards Committee. 1979. *The Public Library Mission Statement and Its Imperatives for Service.* Chicago: American Library Association.

Rawlinson, Nora. 1981. "Give 'Em What They Want!" *Library Journal* 109 (November 15): 2188–90.

Search Institute. 1997. "The Forty Developmental Assets." Available at www.search-institute.org/assets. Last accessed May 18, 2003.

———. 2001. *Step by Step: A Young Person's Guide to Positive Community Change.* Minneapolis, Minn.: Search Institute.

Selznick, Philip. 1957. *Leadership in Administration.* New York: Harper and Row.

Sutherland, Sue. 2001. "Passion, Practice, Partnership and Politics— Marketing the Future of Public Libraries." Available at http://;library,christchurch.org.na/Bibliofile/2001/Passion.pdf. Last accessed November 2002.

Sutton, Roger. 1993. "An Unusual Contribution: The Work of 1993 Grolier Award Winner Mike Printz." *School Library Journal* (September): 154–58.

Tapscott, Don. 1998. *Growing Up Digital: The Rise of the Net Generation.* New York: McGraw-Hill.

"Teen Read Week." 2002. Chicago: American Library Association. Available at www.ala.org/teenread. Last accessed January 4, 2003.

Upon the Objects to Be Attained by the Establishment of a Public Library: Report of the Trustees of the Public Library of the City of Boston. 1852. Boston: Trustees of the Public Library of the City of Boston.

Urban Libraries Council. 2001. PLPYD Youth Voice. "Teens Give Back." Available at http://www.urbanlibraries.org/plpyd/giveback1.html. Last accessed October 7, 2002.

Vaillancourt, Renée J. 2000. *Bare Bones Young Adult Services: Tips for Public Library Generalists.* Chicago: American Library Association.

Van House, Nancy A., et al. 1987. *Output Measures for Public Libraries: A Manual of Standardized Procedures.* Second edition. Chicago: American Library Association.

Van Slyck, Abigail A. 1995. *Free to All: Carnegie Libraries and American Culture 1890–1920.* Chicago: University of Chicago Press.

Wacker, Watts, and Jim Taylor. 2000. *The Visionary's Handbook: Nine Paradoxes That Will Shape the Future of Your Business.* New York: HarperBusiness.

Walter, Virginia A. 1992. *Output Measures for Public Library Service to Children: A Manual of Standardized Procedures.* Chicago: American Library Association.

———. 1995. *Output Measures and More: Planning and Evaluating Public Library Services for Young Adults.* Chicago: American Library Association.

———. 1997. "Becoming Digital: Policy Implications for Library Youth Services." *Library Trends* 45 (spring): 585–601.

———. 1999. "Information Navigators: Final Evaluation Report." Unpublished document submitted to the Santa Monica Public Library.

———. 2002. "Evaluation of Year One Data for the PLA/ALSC Early Literacy Initiative." Unpublished document addressed to the PLA/ALSC's Preschool Literacy Initiative.

Whalen, Samuel P., and Joan Costello. 2002. *Public Libraries and Youth Development: A Guide to Practice and Policy.* Chicago: Chapin Hall Center for Children.

Williams, Patrick. 1988. *The American Public Library and the Problem of Purpose.* New York: Greenwood.

"The World Café." 2003. Available at http://www.theworldcafe.com//. Last accessed February 9, 2003.

Wynn, Joan, et al. 1994. *Children, Families, and Communities: A New Approach to Social Services.* Chicago: Chapin Hall Center for Children.

Yohalem, Nicole, and Karen Pittman. 2003. *Public Libraries Reflect, Retool and Reinvent Their Commitment to Young People: Lessons from the Public Libraries as Partners in Youth Development Initiative.* Washington, D.C.: Forum for Youth Investment.

A Youth Library in Every Community. N.d. Chicago: Young People's Reading Round Table, Division of Libraries for Children and Young People of the American Library Association.

Zeldin, Theodore. 1998, 2000. *Conversation: How Talk Can Change Our Lives.* HiddenSpring/Paulist Press.

Index

VIRGINIA WALTER is currently chair of the Department of Information Studies at UCLA. Before joining the faculty at UCLA in 1990, she worked for more than twenty years in public libraries in California. She is a past president of the Association for Library Services to Children, a division of the ALA. Her other publications for the ALA include *Output Measures for Public Library Service to Children* (1992), *Output Measures and More: Planning and Evaluating Public Library Services for Young Adults* (1995), and *Children and Libraries: Getting It Right* (2001). She received her M.L.S. degree from the University of California, Berkeley, and a Ph.D. in public administration from the University of Southern California.

ELAINE MEYERS is currently manager of children's and teen services at the Phoenix Public Library's Burton Barr Central Library. The former project director of the Public Libraries as Partners in Youth Development initiative, Elaine has worked in public library youth services for the past twenty-five years. She has a master's degree in theater from Catholic University (Washington, D.C.) and an M.L.S. degree from the University of Arizona.